Parrots

By H.W.S. Russell

Photography by: Dr. Herbert R. Axelrod; Glen Axelrod; Joan Balzarini; Michael DeFreitas; Isabelle Francais; Michael Gilroy; Fred Harris; Pam Hutchinson; John Manzione; Horst Muller; K.T.Nemuras; Robert Pearcy; H. Reinhard; San Diego Zoo; Ronald R. Smith; Roger Steele; Carol Thiem; Vogelpark Walsrode.

As parrots and parrot-like birds are becoming more and more popular, a need for information regarding their diet, behavior and breeding habits is on the rise. The Duke of Bedford, author of this work, was highly specialized in this field, and was a great asset to the bird fancy.

To aviculturists, the death of the Duke of Bedford was tragic. The Most Noble H.W.S. Russell, 12th Duke of Bedford was found dead on his estate apparently from a gunshot wound inflicted by himself as he tripped while hunting. To the bird world this was indeed a great loss. The Duke kept a great number of birds at liberty, free flying on his estate, and he managed to keep them in tip-top condition and to breed them. He truly knew how to care for and manage these creatures. Luckily, his knowledge has been preserved and can be passed down in his words.

Although the Duke died some time ago, his management techniques still hold true today. This yearBOOK is a product of the Duke of Bedford's informative accounts of caring for parrot and parrot-like birds and modern chapters on training, diet and exercise. This yearBOOK is intended to be an enlightening study and a helpful guide for the novice parrot keeper. Thanks to the Duke's lifelong devotion to these intelligent and affectionate birds, their beauty can be shared by all.

What are yearBOOKS

Because keeping Parrots as pets is growing at a rapid pace, information on their selection, care and breeding is vitally needed in the marketplace. Books, the usual way information of this sort is transmitted, can be too slow. Sometimes by the book is written and published, the material contained therein is a year or two old...and no new material has been added during that time. Only a book in a magazine form can bring breaking stories and current information. A magazine is streamlined in production, so we have adopted certain magazine publishing techniques in the creation of this yearBOOK. Magazines also can be much cheaper than books because they are supported by advertising. To combine these asstes into a great publication, we issued this yearBOOK in both magazine and book format at different prices.

yearBOOKS,INC.

Dr. Herbert R. Axelrod,
Founder & Chairman

Neal Pronek
Chief Editor

Linda Lindner
Editor

yearBOOKS are all photo composed, color separated and designed on Scitex equipment in Neptune, N.J. with the following staff:

DIGITAL PRE-PRESS
Patricia Northrup
Supervisor

Robert Onyrscuk
Jose Reyes

COMPUTER ART
Patti Escabi
Sandra Taylor Gale
Candida Moreira
Joanne Muzyka
Francine Shulman

ADVERTISING SALES
George Campbell
National Advertising Manager
Amy Manning
Advertising Director
Sandy Cutillo
Advertising Coordinator
Nancy Rivadeneira
*Periodicals Advertising
Sales Manager*
Cheryl Blyth
*Periodicals Sales
Representative*

©yearBOOKS, Inc.
1 TFH Plaza
Neptune, N.J. 07753
Completely manufactured in Neptune, N.J.
USA

Cover design by Sherise Buhagiar

Contents

Introduction

Parrots are becoming more popular in the pet world, and deservedly so; they are very economical to keep, have a long life expectancy, and prove to be very affectionate. Pictured are three macaws posing at the beach.

The parrot family has occupied a deservedly high place in the favor of bird-keepers since ancient Roman times. The intelligence of parrots and their affection for their owners, their power of imitating the human voice, their longevity and gorgeous plumage, all combine to place them high on the list as pets or aviary inmates. There are some people, however, that argue against all of their attributes and feel that the coloring of psittacine birds is gaudy rather than beautiful, that their natural cries are disagreeable, that they are destructive to growing plants, and that they are unpleasant to handle without strong gloves. Today, however, we may reply that for the most part there are many species to

which none of these objections apply, and some to which only one or two can be made.

Aviculture—the keeping, breeding and managing of birds—is yet in its infancy. Much ignorance still prevails and a good many birds in confinement are subjected to unnecessary suffering through the lack of knowledge and thoughtlessness of their owners. Parrots are no exception. It is in order to remedy this state of affairs, as well as to increase the pleasure which may be derived from the study of this fascinating group, that this book has been written.

"Parrots and parrot-like birds" is not a complete monograph of the family, but only an attempt to include the

majority of those species that have been kept as pets in captivity. Many species and a few sub-genera are not mentioned at all. Of these, several are very unlikely to be kept at all outside of their natural environment and others, however, we may hope someday to see in our aviaries.

The writer has made use, as far as possible, of the most recent scientific nomenclature. While this may result in many well-known birds appearing under strange and unfamiliar Latin names, modern classification has at least this merit from an avicultural point of view: that it tends to associate in the same sub-genus only birds that are exceedingly closely allied. The reader will therefore be fairly safe in assuming that when little information is given about a species it is almost identical with better-known and more fully described birds bearing the same sub-generic titles.

Parrots are available in all colors and sizes. In general, the young of any parrot species is a duller version of the adult. These are three young Jendaya Conures that have not achieved their adult coloration.

Cages and Aviaries

There is a wide range of parrot cages available in today's market. Many different sizes and styles that suit the needs of both bird and owner can be found at local pet shops everywhere. Cages are even available that match the decor of your home. With such a wide variety available, there is no reason to keep a bird in cramped quarters.

The size cage you purchase will obviously depend on the species of bird you keep. Smaller parrots such as the lovebirds do not require the same amount of room as Amazon parrots. When your bird sits on a perch in the middle of the cage an allowance of four inches above the bird's head and four inches below its longest tail feather, as well as four inches on each side of its body when its wings are extended is the minimum amount of space needed to house a bird comfortably. No bird should be kept in a cage which does not allow it freely to stretch its wings. A good cage would be large enough to allow its inmate to exercise its wings without hitting the sides of the cage as well as be easy to clean on a daily basis for the owner.

Be certain that the cage you purchase for your bird is strong enough to handle the strength of your bird's beak. The wire that is used on parrot cages comes in many different gauges and a very heavy gauge is needed for a macaw or cockatoo. Many a bird owner has returned home, after thinking his bird was safely locked away, to find his pet parrot out and about chewing on window sills and mouldings. It is also advisable to purchase a good padlock or combination lock for the latch on your cage

A safe, sturdy cage with basic accessories like a perch, removable bottom, and even a swing is a must for your pet parrot. Photo courtesy of Prevue Pet Products, Inc. For the location of a participating pet dealer nearest you call (800) 243-3624.

because many parrots quickly learn how to undo these and let themselves out.

No bird owner will enjoy taking care of his/her pet parrot if the cage it lives in is not easy to care for. Ease of cleaning is therefore an important feature of a good cage. The bottom tray in an average cage for a parrot is made of metal and can be pulled out easily to clean. This will facilitate daily cleaning. With proper care, this tray bottom should last a long time. Each day the tray should be lined with a suitable fresh litter, shavings, corn cob, etc., that can catch and absorb the bird's droppings and dropped food. This litter must be discarded on a daily basis to avoid your pet parrot going down to the bottom and eating or picking through its own feces or spoiled food. It is arguable if the larger parrots require grit as the smaller birds and therefore a small amount of this can be placed in a flat dish on top of the shavings on the floor of the cage.

In addition to the bottom tray, easy access to food and water containers, preferably from the outside, is essential. You never know when you may need the assistance of a friend or neighbor to feed your pet parrot, and it is much better for them and your bird, if they do not have to struggle to get to the feeding dishes.

The cage bars should be situated so that your bird can climb about easily and not have trouble getting from one place in the cage to the next. These bars should also be easy to wipe clean with a cloth. Birds are incredibly talented at getting all sorts of food substances all over the wire bars of the cage, making

Bird cages need to be lined so they can be cleaned quickly and easily. Bird owners have a variety of substrates to choose from courtesy of EcoClean™. For the location of a pet dealer nearest you call (800) 537-3370.

Be sure to purchase a bird cage that is large enough to house your pet parrot comfortably and that allows plenty of room for toys and accessories as well.

them rather sticky. Also, birds with a lot of powder down, such as cockatoos, can't help but get this powder all over the cage. Keeping the cage clean is beneficial to the health of your bird.

A very large trade is done by dealers who sell a parrot and cage at an "attractive" price. This is wonderful for the prospective buyer for he is able to purchase a good-sized cage along with his new pet parrot. The parrot is thus well equipped from the beginning of its new lifestyle and will be off to a good start. Most pet shop dealers are very knowledgeable in parrots and can recommend the proper type of cage for the species you are interested in. If the bird you are interested in requires a cage larger than you had allotted space for in your home, do not do the bird injustice and cramp it into a smaller cage. Please change your mind on the species of bird and purchase a smaller

one instead. Smaller parrots can make just as exciting and fun pets as the larger species.

There is no need to cover your parrot's cage with a cloth for the night. The cage should only be covered if you are afraid of the parrot becoming chilled. Birds should not be kept in a draft in the first place, so there is really no need for a cover. You may, however, find that your parrot is rather chatty and noisy at nighttime and a cover may be the only way to quiet the bird down.

In addition to food and water, your parrot should be supplied with branches from non-toxic trees, perches, toys and a bath. Place the bath, if possible, in such a position that the droppings from the perch do not fall into it. If a parrot is slow in taking an interest in any of these, or any type of food, that would be beneficial to it, do not be dis-

couraged, but continue to offer them at regular intervals, for months if need be. Sooner or later they are pretty sure to be patronized. Some birds are just stubborn.

Many parrots which do not bathe on their own love to be placed under a light shower or to be sprayed with tepid water. Never force a shower bath on a bird that not only objects to the first few drops that fall on it, but continues

It is practical to have a spare cage on hand that is easy to transport and that is comfortable for your parrot in case he ever falls ill or you are traveling with your bird. Photo courtesy of Bird Motel/Papagallo Enterprises. For the location of a pet dealer nearest you call (219) 436-9730.

to object after a minute has passed. A new item on the bird market is a shower perch for birds. Such a perch is designed to attach to your own shower. It is a welcome addition to the bird accessory market because it is no more messy than you taking a shower yourself! Some owners even wind up showering at the same time their bird does. Be sure you always use tepid water not hot, otherwise your parrot could be seriously injured.

To disinfect your parrot's cage, remove the bird and thoroughly brush on a solution of bleach and water. Allow this to sit for a few minutes and then rinse very well with warm water. Be sure to wash all feeding dishes and perches in the same way and rinse and allow to dry thoroughly.

There is nothing more aggravating than a cage that is not easy to clean. It truly makes the task of caring for your bird an unpleasant experience and makes the bird a nervous wreck! Be sure to purchase the best possible cage for your bird so that you can enjoy a long life with your new pet.

AVIARIES

There are two types of outdoor aviaries which can be considered really satisfactory to contain parrots—movable aviaries and permanent. A permanent aviary will have the floor made of brick, concrete, or similar hard material that can be easily washed and disinfected. A less costly and easy to disassemble type of aviary has an earthen floor to the flight, however, this tends to get steadily more destructive the longer it stands. Of course, if you like, you can keep such an aviary, however, you would need to replace the floor dirt every so often. This type of flooring is also not very sanitary and is very difficult to sterilize.

A rectangular movable aviary, gives very good results with the health of most parrots that are kept within. The aviary, including the floor, is covered with a strong half–inch mesh wire netting and the wooden framework of the flight is on the outside of the wire and not on the inside. The object of covering the floor is to exclude rats and other burrowing animals. Grass quickly grows through the mesh and makes the wire invisible. The advantage of having the wooden framework on the outside is that the birds cannot bite it, nor can they sit on it and soil it with their droppings.

In the top left–hand corner of such an aviary flight should be a small hinged door that opens inward and upward. This door can be propped open at any time when the bird is to be set at liberty; it should have a fastening on the outside as well as on the inside or else a playful bird may learn to open it. The same door can be used when the catching box is brought into operation. This catching box is a rectangular box of wire netting with an inside lining of taut string netting to keep the birds from knocking themselves against the wire and hurting their heads and nostrils. It is made to hook to the top of the aviary in front of the small top corner door and it is itself fitted with a wooden door, corresponding in size to the aperture of the top door, which slides in a groove from left to right. When you wish to catch a bird, hook the catching box onto the aviary, push back the slide of the catching box, undo the fastenings of the little top door, and tie one end of string round the base of the top door (the top door should be of wire on a wooden frame). Pass the other end of the string through a mesh of the wire in the aviary roof so as to supply leverage for pulling the top door open against the roof of the aviary. Then take your stand about half way back in the aviary flight, still holding the string in your hand, and then either yourself, or with the help of an assistant, gently drive the bird you wish to capture into the catching box. As soon as it enters the box, slacken the string you are holding and the top door, if properly oiled and working freely, as it should be before you start operations, falls downward of its own weight, making the bird a prisoner. You then mount a pair of steps, push forward and fasten the slide of the catching box, close and fasten the top door, and the capture is safely effected without any chasing about with a net. It is very important in the hurry of the moment, not to forget the catching box slide. If you do, as soon as you unhook the catching box the bird darts out to freedom and the catching has to be done over again–under much more difficult circumstances! Of course a very wary bird may refuse to enter the catching box, especially if it has been caught in it before; in that case, other methods have to be adopted. When a net is used, always cover the rim with thick, soft padding.

In the left–hand corner of the front of the aviary flight should be an entrance door. In the center of the front of the aviary flight a small door.

The wire roof at the front end of the aviary flight may be covered with corrugated metal to give some protection from sun and rain, and further protection is afforded by other sheets of corrugated metal which cover the shelter and project about two feet over the shelter end of the flight.

In addition, a flat circular piece of wood can be fixed on the outside of the center of the wire roof of the aviary flight. Four perches diverging to the

four corners of the aviary flight are fastened at one end to a stout piece of wood being attached to the circular shelter disc above, as the stalk of a mushroom is attached to the umbrella portion. The other end of the left–hand front perch runs up to the bottom end of the little top door in the left–hand corner, thus leading a bird up to the catching box when the door is open.

The aviary shelter itself should be at least 2.5 ft deep from back to front and the same height as the flight. In

Sturdy, well built, roomy, and especially attractive, Kings Aviary cages prove to be excellent housing facilities for your pet parrot. For the location of a participating dealer nearest you call (516)777-7300.

the center of the front of the shelter is a small window. In the right–hand side of the shelter is a small door 1ft. square on the inside of which is fixed a stout bit of wire to hold the seed dish and another to hold a small receptacle for water which is only needed when birds are confined to the shelter and have not access to the bath in the flight.

The shelter has three perches that run from back to front and so arranged that no droppings fall into the seed

dish. One of these perches leads up to the entrance hole and a corresponding perch in the flight also leads up to the entrance hole so that the birds do not have to jump up and jump down when passing through.

The floor of the shelter should be of metal and sufficiently strong for the person cleaning out the aviary to treat on it without causing damage. It should be thickly covered with dry sand. On no account use damp sand, as this is liable to cause chills.

The roof of the shelter should be made water-proof and mouseproof with corrugated metal on top. The corrugated metal should protect somewhat into the flight so as to overhang the cross perch in the flight, already mentioned as being nine inches from the front of the aviary shelter. The aviary shelter itself should always be boarded with tongue–and–grooved lumber. Where hard–biting birds are kept, such as the bigger broadtails, Ringnecks, and parrots, the wood-work of the front of the aviary shelter must be covered with wire netting, but for the smaller broad-tails and Asiatic parakeets, lovebirds, etc., this is unnec-essary. In the case of cocka-toos, pileated parakeets, and other hard–biting birds, an inner layer of very strong wire netting of the thickest possible gauge must be used throughout the aviary inside the fine mesh wire netting, an outer covering of which is required to exclude mice.

Training and Environment

Captive-bred parrots know nothing except being handled, cuddled and loved since practically out of the egg! This is a baby Black Palm Cockatoo being hand fed. Note the horn color of the bird's beak, when this bird matures the beak will turn black.

Most parrots that are available today have been raised in captivity. Many of these captive-bred birds have been taken from their parents at a very young age and hand fed by humans. These birds know nothing of what it is to be wild; they only know cuddling, handling and love from practically right out of the egg! For one of these birds to bite or act aggressive something disastrous must be happening to it. Training a bird of this sort is very easy as a parrot has great pleasure in pleasing its owner. Captive-bred birds enjoy their owners, and the affection that they display proves this fact.

Many captive-bred birds can be taught to ride on roller skates, skateboards, fly through hoops and do a number of other crazy antics. To do this type of training a more in-depth guide should be sought, and companies that produce all the paraphernalia for such usually supply training guides and instructional video tapes.

WING-CLIPPING

There are captive-bred birds that have never been handled as well as ones that have not been handled since they were weaned off hand feeding. These birds require basic training in order to be handled. Basic training is more easily accomplished if the bird has its wing or wings clipped.

Wing clipping, when done correctly, is a painless procedure that takes a matter of minutes. Only feathers are cut, and this is about as painful as a haircut. Birds only react negatively to the procedure because they must be restrained in order to carry out the task. Very tame birds will allow their owners to hold out their wing and clip the necessary feathers away with no need of restraint. If you have never clipped a bird's wing, do not attempt this yourself. Bring your bird to a veterinarian or an establishment that has experienced people to do the job.

There are several advantages in clipping a bird's wing. First, and probably most beneficial, a bird cannot be lost out a window or door. Secondly, it cannot fly around your home and accidentally fall into something cooking on the stove or fly into a mirror or window and gravely injure

Like most living creatures, birds enjoy some private time as well as social time, and retreat areas are welcome in their cages. Photo courtesy of Niche Pet Products, Inc./Happy Hut. For the location of a participating dealer near you call (800) 316-0000.

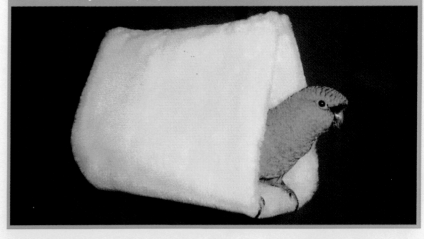

Some birds are so tame that they allow their owner to clip their wing without the need of restraint. This Grey Parrot demonstrates how easy wing clipping can be!

itself. A third advantage is that a clipped bird is more easily tamed than an unclipped one because more time can be spent actually handling the bird instead of chasing it around the house.

HAND TAMING

To tame your unhandleable bird, be certain that its wings are clipped, remove it from its cage, and work with it close to the floor in a corner where it cannot get away from you behind furniture. Attempt to have it step up onto your other hand, or arm (depending on the size of the bird). After several successful steps, try to scratch the top of the bird's head by beginning under its beak and working your way around to the back of the neck and up the top of the head. If the bird is too nervous to step up onto your hand, you may use two perches instead of your hands. Gradually you can move your hands closer on the perches and eventually the bird will be standing on your hand.

Taming sessions should only last 20 minutes and should always end on a positive note. If a taming session is not going well, go back to something the bird does do well and then put it back in its cage. Never put a bird that is not behaving the way you want it to back in its cage; this will only make the next taming session harder.

SPEECH TRAINING

Speech training is altogether different than hand taming. A bird need not be hand tame to learn to mimic speech. A hand tame bird, however, does pay more attention to its owner than a non-tame one, and attention is needed to speech train.

Speech training is purely a matter of repetition. If you were to say good morning every morning when you entered your bird's room, your bird would certainly learn to repeat it back to you! Teach your bird one word at a time. Start off with single syllable words, and work your way to multiple syllables, multiple words, and sentences. Be sure you have your bird's full attention, and always reward it with a food tidbit or a scratch on the head.

EXERCISE

All birds require exercise to maintain a healthy lifestyle. Some birds are able to achieve a good amount of daily exercise in their cages, however, the average parrot cage does not offer enough room to do so. Free time away from the cage is the best way to ensure that your bird receives the proper amount of exercise. Aside from physical exercise, free time also provides your bird with plenty of mental exercise.

There is much a parrot can enjoy while spending time away from its cage, and there are many hidden dangers as well. As a responsible parrot owner you must watch your bird closely while it is free roaming. All electrical cords, outlets, houseplants, cats, dogs, open fish tanks, fireplaces, etc. are all possible dangers that pet parrots perceive as fun. Don't let your parrot fall victim to a careless accident.

Toys

Toys are another form of exercise and these can be within the cage or on a playgym outside of the cage. They are available in many

Like people and other animals, birds need mental as well as physical stimulation and toys that are also games can provide a great deal. Photo courtesy of Jungle Talk® International; Call (800)738-8697 for the location of the participating pet dealer nearest you.

Colors, shapes and flavors all enhance a toy's appeal to a parrot. Photo courtesy of Jungle Talk® International; call (800) 738-8697 for the location of the participating pet dealer nearest you.

different colors, and sizes and prove beneficial to a parrot's mental health. Parrots of all kinds need toys. Big parrots, little parrots, mid-sized parrots—they all need toys. Certain other pet birds need toys also, but no other group seems to derive as much pleasure from toys, or as great a sense of deprivation if they don't have them, as parrots. Perhaps that's because parrots are comparatively more intelligent than most other birds, or perhaps it's a result of parrots' greater degree of sociability or their advanced tactile sense. We don't really know for sure. What we do know for sure is that parrots use toys and seem to derive amusement and pleasure from them, sometimes even a great deal of amusement and pleasure. Once you've seen your bird pulling and dragging and turning and chewing and lifting and carrying a favorite toy for hours on end, you'll lose any doubt you ever had about the attraction

parrots have for toys.

The question then becomes pretty much the same thing as it is in offering toys to children: what kind of toys should be offered? Obviously some articles are suited to use as toys and some are not. In general, the most important consideration in choosing proper toys is the safety of the bird or birds intended to use them. Whatever else toys should be, they definitely shouldn't be dangerous. Danger, unfortunately, comes in a number of different forms, not all of them immediately recognizable. Danger can come from the size of the toy (some are too small for safe usage by large parrots, which might swallow them whole), from what it is made of or covered with (toxic materials can kill quickly, and you usually can't tell whether a material is toxic just by looking at it or smelling it), from what it's attached to (items that dangle can also strangle) and a few other things.

Normally the most dangerous toys are

items that were never intended to be used as parrot toys, household articles that get pressed into service because they happen to be handy. Keep in mind that the fact that a bird is interested in—even seemingly fascinated by—a particular item doesn't mean that that item is safe to play with. Conversely, the safest toys for parrots are items that have been specifically designed as parrot toys. There is a wide variety of such toys offered for sale, made in a wide enough range of sizes and materials to allow you to pick out the toys that are right for your birds. You might have to do some experimenting, because parrots, especially the larger parrots, are very variable in their likes and dislikes for particular toys; what entrances one parrot may leave another bird of the same species completely uninterested.

The major function of a parrot toy is to keep its user

Parrots enjoy toys that are colorful, durable and that include a variety of materials with which to interact. Photo courtesy of Fellner's Fine Feathered Friends. Call (800)965-0080 for your nearest dealer.

Birds that become bored and that do not have enough mental stimulation, either with toys or interaction with people, sometimes develop destructive habits. This Grey Parrot has plucked his own feathers and is practically bare! A lot of baths, toys, and time out of its cage, along with a well balanced diet will probably correct his habit.

In their natural environments, birds have a variety of surfaces upon which to use their beaks. Owners can give their birds toys that simulate natural conditions. Photo courtesy of Good Bird™ Toys. For the name and location of a pet dealer nearest you call (313) 769-1301.

Birds enjoy looking at different surroundings. During the day, take your parrot with you to different spots of your home or yard so that it too can enjoy the day. Portable perches, or stands that make moving from one room to the next are available at your local pet store.

from becoming bored, because boredom can lead to many different forms of destructive behavior. Feather plucking is just one example of a type of bad behavior that is a possible result of boredom in a pet parrot; biting and general bad-temperedness as well as listlessness and resistance to training are others. But another important function of parrot toys is to provide pleasure to parrot owners. Theses owners often seem to get more enjoyment from watching their birds with the toys they've chosen for them than the birds get from the toys themselves.

ENVIRONMENT

The environment in which you keep your bird is very

Household items are not always safe for your pet parrot to play with, many have hidden dangers. Be certain that the items you give to your bird cannot cause any harm.

important to its health. No bird should be kept in a drafty area. Drafts ultimately lead to a cold or something worse. Conversely, placing your bird in front of a sunny window can be detrimental to its health. If you have ever spent time in direct sunlight you know that there are periods of extreme heat (when the sun is out) and cooler periods (when the sun goes behind a cloud). The periods of warmth are much more intense through a window. It is because of these great temperature differences that it is not wise to keep your parrot in front of a sunny window.

The best place to keep your parrot is in a quiet corner of the house. A corner does not allow movement to come from behind or the side of your bird and frighten it.

Birds can experience terrible night fright. They can injure themselves horribly by banging into the sides of the cage wire. In the middle of the night they cannot see what they are hitting and just keep hitting the sides of the cage until finally they are just too exhausted to move. By this time they are usually injured very badly. To avoid this from happening, a small light should be left on at night to allow your bird to see should something frighten it.

BATHS

Regular baths will keep your parrot's plumage in really great condition. A bath can be anything from your parrot's drinking cup to a sprinkling with tepid water in your sink or shower. Whatever is used as a bathing facility be certain that your pet does not catch a chill afterward. On hot summer days your parrot will appreciate being taken outside and sprayed with a light hose. Never continue a bath if your bird tries to avoid the water. A bird that wants a bath will

Variety, durability and safe materials are all essential elements of desirable and long-lasting toys for your parrot. Photo courtesy of Twiggle Toys/Nest Egg Manufacturing. For the name and location of a pet dealer nearest you call (209) 524-2828.

Birds of all types enjoy baths. If you do not provide something for your bird to bathe in, it will choose one itself. This cockatiel is attempting to bathe in a coffee mug!

fluff out its feathers and spread its wings wide. It will thoroughly enjoy itself. In addition to plain water, there are many bird bath sprays available from your local pet store that will add sheen and luster to your bird's feathers.

A happy parrot is one who can climb, chew and maneuver to get the exercise he needs. Photo courtesy of Pet-Ag®/Pink Parrot®; (800) 323-6878.

Diet

In the wild, parrots forage about for their food. They eat seeds from plants and trees, fruits and berries, bugs, grubs and insects, and even some dirt and clay. In a days time they consume vitamins, carbohydrates, proteins, fats, amino acids, and salts and minerals—a well balanced diet.

The term "parrots" is general and encompasses a large number of different bird species. All these species have different dietary requirements. In order for birds to remain in good health and feather they must receive a properly balanced diet. However, being that the group of parrots is so large, they do not all have the same requirements, and cannot all be fed in the same way. Even within birds of the same genus, such as cocka-toos, the dietary needs differ,

An assortment of vegetables keeps parrots looking and feeling their best, and peppers add zest to the variety. Photo courtesy of Eight In One Pet Products, Inc. For the location of the participating pet dealer nearest you call (516)232-1200.

although this is slight, they still differ. In the wild, it is easy for birds to consume what they need to thrive, but in captivity they rely on their owners. Not having access to the same seeds, nuts, berries, grubs, etc., as the birds do in the wild, bird owners must rely on bird food manufacturing companies to provide a well-balanced bird diet that simulates what their pets would receive in the wild. Luckily for owners, these manufacturing companies have spent years of research in creating such diets.

The diet for your pet parrot must be nutritionally inclu-

sive. Bird food manufacturing companies have been successful in including all of a parrots nutritional requirements in a diet that is pleasing to a parrot's palate and relatively simple for the bird owner to administer.

Commercially prepared parrot foods are designed to maintain the health and well-being of these birds. Photo courtesy of Pretty Pets International; Call (800)356-5020 for the name and location of the participating pet dealer nearest you.

Careful vitamin supplementation ensures that your caged companion gets all the nutrients he or she needs. Photo courtesy of Jungle Talk® International; call (800) 738-8697 for the location of the participating pet dealer nearest you.

As a parrot owner it is your duty to supply your pet with a proper diet. You will also benefit from giving your bird its nutritional needs because your pet will be a happier and healthier specimen. An inadequate diet results in lack of resistance to many illnesses, lack of stamina, and poor feather condition. Many disorders, that were originally believed to be psychological, can be directly related to improper diets. It is easy to see why a proper diet is so important. It is therefore important that you receive specific information regarding your parrot's diet from a breeder of that species or a well informed establishment. This chapter will briefly describe basic dietary needs for parrots in general. Certain bird species and their particular seed likes and dislikes are listed in later chapters.

All parrots require health grit for minerals, cuttlebone for calcium and salt, and greenfood and softfood for vitamins and variety. Of course, a constant supply of water should be available to all birds in captivity, as water is necessary to all forms of life.

Whether you own one bird or an aviary full of birds, a vitamin supplement is a necessity. Many vitamin supplements are available at your local pet store in a variety of forms. Liquid preparations are most popular, but check which one will best suit the needs of the species you keep.

The key to ensuring a well-balanced diet for your stock is variety. If you offer your birds a little bit of many different items, they will be able to pick and eat what they like, and ultimately what they need to

Fruits, vegetables, nuts and various seeds are all needed by your pet parrot to thrive. Krazy Krunch has a variety of sticks that supply these basics and that prove to be fun for your parrot to eat. Photo courtesy of Pet-Ag®/Pink Parrot®; call (800)323-6878 for the name and location of a pet dealer near you.

thrive. People food is also permissible in small quantities, as long as what is being offered is good for you.

Of course, not all parrot owners can afford the time or the money to prepare a delicious fresh vegetable assortment as what is in front of this cockatoo. If you are preparing such a meal for yourself, be certain to pass some to your bird.

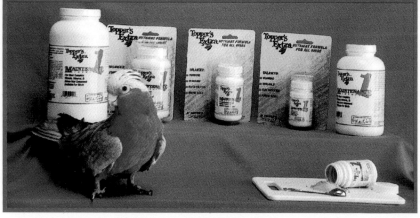

The best we can do for our captive feathered companions is give them the range of nutrients they would have available in the wild, judiciously supplemented with special vitamins. Photo courtesy of Topper's™ Extra. For the location and name of a pet dealer nearest you call (209)524-2828.

Kaytee offers specially blended mixes for the species and age of bird you keep. These are always fresh and supply your bird with the nutrients needed for it to thrive. Photo courtesy of Kaytee. Call (800)KAYTEE-1 for information or the pet dealer nearest you.

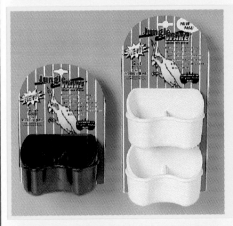

You may find you need several seed dishes for the different foods your parrot will want or need to eat. Photo courtesy of Jungle Talk® International; call (800) 738-8697 for the location of the participating pet dealer nearest you.

When your parrot has a craving for human-quality fruits and nuts and needs the nutrients available in bee pollen, it's nice to know they are readily available. Photo courtesy of Noah's Kingdom; call (800)662-4711 for information or the pet dealer nearest you.

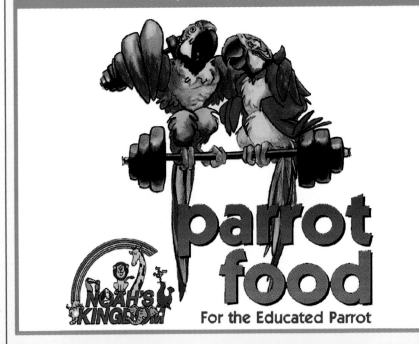

Cooked rice, boiled potatoes, cheese, fruits and vegetables are all good to give your birds. Too much salt or overly spicy foods, however, is not good for you, and neither is it good for your birds. Be wise in what you choose to feed your birds and always feed all table foods in moderation.

Since parrots are inclined to gnaw on anything they can get their beaks on, supply your birds with plenty of fresh twigs from non-toxic trees, and other branches that are sold in pet stores specifically to satisfy their need to gnaw. If twigs and branches are not supplied, your birds will look to other things to gnaw upon, seed dishes, perches, toys, and sometimes even to themselves. They really become destructive if no outlet for this need to gnaw is given. Gnawing on items also gives their beaks exercise and proves to be very therapeutic.

Lovebirds, Cockatiels and Small Parrots

A diet for these small parrots should consist mainly of white millet, and canary seed, as well as oat groats, sunflower, and safflower. Canary seed is high in protein and at least 35% of the bird's diet should consist of it. White millet can be given in the same percentage rate, and 5-10% of the diet should be oat groats. The remaining 20-25% should be made up of the other ingredients in equal parts to each other.

Fresh fruits and vegetables cut up into small pieces will be relished by these little birds, Variety is important and you will soon find out what your bird prefers.

Larger Parrots

The African parrots, Amazon parrots, conures, cockatoos and macaws, can receive the same ingredients as those stated for the small ones with further additions such as raw unsalted peanuts, pumpkin seeds, and some grains such as wheat, milo, and corn. Parrot mixes on the market may also contain turkey mash crumbles and top grade dry kibbled dog food. These birds too will enjoy a wide variety of fresh fruits and vegetables.

BREEDING DIET

Breeding birds of all species require greater amounts of calcium and softfood in their diet than non-breeding birds. Calcium is needed by the hen to produce eggs as well as give her enough stamina to rear and raise chicks. Softfood,

Parrots enjoy many fruits, including papaya, pineapple, coconut, cranberries, and raisins. Photo courtesy of Eight In One Pet Products, Inc. Call (516)232-1200 for the name and location of a pet dealer near you.

hard-boiled eggs, corn nibblets, scrambled eggs, tofu, etc., is needed by the parent birds to consume, partially digest, and regurgitate back to their chicks. The softfood, is easier to digest than seeds for both the parents and the chicks.

Be very careful of the amount of vitamins you give to your stock at this time. Too much will harm the chicks. If you feed your birds a properly balanced diet, there is no need to increase the amount of daily supplement. Stick to the usual amount given unless otherwise directed by a veterinarian.

PURCHASING BIRD FOOD

Pet stores and bird specialty shops are fully stocked with a wide arrangement of specially prepared diets for the different species of parrots. As stated earlier, bird food manufacturing companies have spent years researching and testing to come up with correct formulated diets to suit your bird's nutritional requirements. Nearly all types of seed mixes found in pet stores today prove to be beneficial to the well being of your bird. Check with the clerk or bird breeder as to which one will best suit your bird's needs.

Scientifically formulated and balanced avian diets that are made with only the finest and freshest ingredients are designed for your parrot. For more information or the pet dealer nearest you call (800) 878-2666.

Parrots enjoy a combination of seeds, nuts and fruits, and fortunately they're available in a range of treat and regular diet combinations. Photo courtesy of Vitakraft Pet Products Co., Inc.; call (800)237-3324 for the location of a participating pet dealer near you.

For a neater cage—and therefore a healthier bird—make sure you have various food bowls in which you can place the variety of foods parrots like. Photo courtesy of Pearce Plastics Corp.; (818)797-8481.

You'll know your parrot is eating a nutritious diet if he radiates good health. Photo courtesy of ZuPreem; call (800)345-4767 for the location of the participating pet dealer nearest you.

No matter what manufactured brand you use, it is important that it is fresh. The freshness of a seed can easily be checked by germinating it. If after 48 hours of soaking in water the seed has not sprouted, it is not fresh. Webby seed can be a problem to bird owners and pet shop dealers. This does not mean that it is not fresh. Fresh seed can be webby. In hot temperatures the larval stage, or caterpillar, of the tiny seed moth spins a web clinging to seed. There is no harm in this web, and if the birds eat the caterpillars they will add a trace of animal protein to the diet. The seed moth does become pesky and to avoid this it is best to keep the seed cool. Seed only becomes a danger to birds if it should become wet and moldy so avoid this at all costs.

WATER

All birds require water to survive. Water must be supplied fresh each day and always be available. If your bird chooses to bathe immediately after you fill its water cup in the morning, fill it again after the bath is over.

Never allow your bird to be without water. Birds are very vulnerable to dehydration and must always have a constant supply of water.

Spring or bottled water is best to give you bird because it is always the same and it is always pure. Tap water, unfortunately, is always different, especially in the summer. When the tempera-

tures are high, bacteria easily grows in our reservoirs. Chlorine and other chemicals are then added into our water system to kill the bacteria, yet these prove harmful to our birds if they consume too much. This is why bottled water is best, and to avoid a digestive disorder or a case of diarrhea, stick with the spring or bottled water all year round.

Treats that are fun to eat as well as nutritious are available from your local pet store. Photo courtesy of Kaytee. Call (800) KAYTEE-1 for the pet dealer nearest you.

African Parrots

AFRICAN GREY PARROT —
PSITTACUS ERITHACUS ERITHACUS

Distribution: Equatorial Africa

Adult male: Ash grey, paler on the rump and abdomen. Flight feathers dark grey. Tail and tail-coverts red. Bill blackish. Irises pale yellow. Length 13 inches. Size about that of a pigeon.

Adult female: Similar to the male but smaller with a less massive head and beak. The bare skin at the back of the eye is said to be more rounded and less elliptical in shape.

Immature: Differs in having the tail dark red towards the tip and the under tail-coverts dark red, tinged with grey. Irises dark grey.

The Grey Parrot has been a well-known favorite for a great number of years, and many stories are told of its intelligence and linguistic powers. It is, par excellence, the bird for those who want a house pet to amuse them with its mimicry of the human voice. Not only does it adapt itself wonderfully to cage life, and with proper treatment survive for an immense number of years, but as a talker it has few rivals and no superior. Moreover, if some of its whistling

cries are unpleasantly shrill, it never, unless terrified, can be properly said to screech. It is also of a more equable temperament than the Blue-fronted Amazon. Few amazons can be trusted in moments of mischievous excitement to refrain from nipping the fingers of even their best friends, but a Grey Parrot is seldom treacherous. Once he has really given you his heart he is always gentle except under great provocation, but anyone, especially a stranger, who is foolish enough to make advances that are not welcome, does so at his own peril and has no reason to complain if, as is extremely likely, he receives a severe bite.

The Grey Parrot should be fed on a seed mixture made especially for larger parrots as

When choosing a pet Grey Parrot, it is best to select only one bird. Two birds would keep each other company, however, they would pay attention to each other rather than you.

well as sweet, soft fruits like grapes and ripe pears. Apples are eaten if they are of the best dessert kinds and in good condition. A Grey has a very discriminating palate, and usually rejects apples if they are soft, sour, or ill-flavored. A very small bit of plain cake does no harm as a tidbit, as well as other table foods fed in moderate amounts. Very young Grey Parrots will sometimes eat only boiled maize (corn), a food which must be prepared fresh daily, but they can usually be induced to take soaked seed and, in due course, dry seed. Sunflower soaked until the shell is quite soft is very attractive to young parrots, but the water in which seed is soaking must be

The Grey Parrot learns to mimic the human voice very well. It is important that you have the bird's full attention in order for it to learn well.

When you want to pet your Grey Parrot, allow the bird to see your hand and begin petting it on its wing, work your way up the bird's neck and around to the back of it's head. Never reach directly over the bird's head because this will frighten it and it will then be afraid of hands.

the majority of cases undoubtedly they do not, but it is almost equally certain that the more intelligent birds do so in some instances. A Grey Parrot is also quick to associate ideas by sight or sound. A hen bird in my possession imitates the blowing of a nose either on being shown a handkerchief or on hearing a sneeze. The pouring out of water also evokes from her a realistic gurgling noise which says more for her quickness and mind than for the table manners of her former associates. Very young parrots have grey irises but the color soon changes to the pale yellow eye of the adult. There is not the slightest evidence that Gray Parrots take nearly 20 years to become sexually mature. In

a wild state they almost undoubtedly begin to breed approximately their fourth year and possibly one or even two years sooner.

The Grey Parrot has been bred both at liberty, in aviaries, and in close confinements. A genuine male is usually a very big, rather gaunt-looking fellow, with, according to some authorities, the bare grey patch behind the eye less rounded and more elliptical in shape. If tame, he is generally a brilliant talker, though most hens also talk well, only a very few being unable to learn anything. If a true pair can be obtained, Grey Parrots are really easier to breed than some parakeets, for the males retain their fertility with very

changed daily or it will become very offensive.

Grey Parrots are not regular bathers, but appreciate an occasional spray or rain bath. The dry streaky plumage of the numerous unfortunate birds whose owners never allow them to bathe contrast very unfavorable with the appearance of well-cared-for specimens.

A Grey Parrot should have a piece of wood to occupy its beak, but on no account should it be allowed to bite anything painted or varnished. Hen Grey Parrots in breeding condition spend a lot of time scratching up the sand at the bottom of the cage, as they would do when excavating a tree trunk hollow.

It is often asked whether or not parrots understand the meaning of what they say. In

As your Grey Parrot ages the white part of its eye ring will turn yellow. Once it reaches this stage, it is difficult to judge the age of the bird, and therefore accurate records should be kept.

The Senegal Parrot is quite playful and learns to talk very well. It is a medium-sized bird with a stocky build and, because of its strong beak, must be housed in a cage with a fairly heavy gauge.

little wing exercise, and a good hollow log or barrel partly filled with decayed wood makes a satisfactory nursery for the young. A pair, when first introduced is very slow to make friends, but once mated, become savage and aggressive towards humans. If you want a parrot to be a pet, *don't* get it a partner! Single hen birds frequently lay eggs and may become egg-bound. Be certain to watch this very carefully when she is known to be laying.

The Grey Parrot is subject to color variation. Birds with an abnormal quantity of pink feathers are not uncommon, also partial albinos; pure albinos with red tails occur, and, rarest of all, wholly white specimens and grey birds with white tails. I once had the transient pleasure of owning a red-tailed albino which a dealer transferred to me for a heroic figure. As the bird was

very young and was suffering from parrot fever, its mortal remains soon graced a Scottish museum.

Old writers sometimes refer to the Grey Parrot as the Jaco.

SENEGAL PARROT—
POICEPHALUS SENEGALUS

Distribution: Gambia

Adult male: Green. Head dark greyish, paler on the cheeks. Lower breast and abdomen orange-yellow. Flights dusky with a green tinge on the outer webs. Tail is short and greenish brown in color. Bill is black. Length 9+ inches.

Adult female: Similar but with a much narrower and finer head.

A popular and well-known bird and probably one of the best of the small parrots for anyone who requires a caged pet. The Senegal becomes much attached to one person or to one sex and is lively and playful, learning to say a few words or short sentences. Its chief failings are a slate-pencil

Parrots enjoy and thrive on the companionship of their human partners. They really enjoy being petted and played with, and can accompany you anywhere.

screech and a tendency to bite in moments of mischievous excitement, but not all individuals possess this vice.

The food should consist of a mixture suitable for the smaller parrots with plenty of fruit if the bird's digestion remains in good order.

Senegals are now bred quite freely in captivity.

A young Senegal Parrot does not have the brilliancy of coloration that an adult does.

NYASA LOVEBIRD—*AGAPORNIS LILIANAE*

Distribution: Zambia to Northern Rhodesia and Southernmost part of Tanzania.

Adult male: Forepart of head orange-red, cheeks and throat slightly paler and merging into pink. Back of head yellow merging into green. Remainder of plumage green, slightly paler on the

The Nyasa Lovebird closely resembles the Peach-faced Lovebird, and is the smallest species with a white eye ring.

breast. Bill red. A white circle around the eye. Total length 4 inches. Size about that of a budgerigar.

Adult female: Resembles the male. According to some authorities has a slightly broader beak.

Immature: Slightly less richly colored than the adult.

Unknown to aviculture until recent times, this pretty little lovebird has now become one of the most common aviary birds in many parts of the world, threatening to rival even the budgerigar in popularity. It is easily kept in any kind of aviary, birdroom or flight cage. The main occupation of its existence is rearing numerous progeny, clutch after clutch of eggs being laid with only a pause of a few weeks for the molt. The only check on its fertility in captivity lies in the circumstances that the unhatched embryos are somewhat intolerant of a dry environment, while in cold weather a proportion of the hens are subject to egg-binding. Some aviculturists claim to have overcome the former difficulty, by breeding Nyasas under cover, and providing nest boxes with a false bottom filled with sponge or sphagnum moss kept soaking wet and separated from the mass of twigs in the bark composing the actual nest by a piece of wire gauze. Lime and elm twigs make the best nesting material and the supply must be renewed even after the young are hatched. The cock Nyasa feeds his sitting mate and spends a good deal of time with her in the nest. The difficulty of distinguishing the sexes by their appearance is largely made up for by the facility in which true pairs can be recognized by their behavior. No self-respecting hen Nyasa dreams of delaying to go to nest at the earliest possible moment. If after the lapse of a few weeks, no eggs have appeared, you may be sure your birds are cocks, while double clutches of from eight to ten infertile eggs are equally certain proof that you have nothing but hens.

Nyasa Lovebirds are quite hardy, but their winter treatment in outdoor aviaries presents some difficulty. On the whole it is best to move the nests into the aviary shelter during the autumn and heat the shelter, resigning oneself to a proportion of useless clutches until the warm weather returns.

The Nyasa Lovebird is reported to be fairly quiet in mixed company, and although it agrees well with its owns kind, do not trust it with budgerigars or finches, as some individuals can be very savage.

The food should consist of a mixture of two parts canary, two parts millet, one part oats, one part hemp, and one part sunflower. Green food will be very much relished when offered.

The species interbreeds freely with nearly allied lovebirds; the hybrid with the Black-cheek is rather pretty and perfectly fertile.

FISCHER'S LOVEBIRD— *AGAPORNIS FISCHERI*

Distribution: Northern Tanzania, Lake Victoria and Nzega.

Adult male: General plumage green, paler on the breast.

A band of bright orange-red across the forehead; the same color in a paler shade on the cheeks and throat where it merges into rose color and old-gold. Head and back of neck strongly washed with dull olive green. A patch of dark blue above the root of the tail. Tail feathers green, tipped with blue. Bill bright red. A white circle around the eye. Total length 5+ inches. Somewhat larger than the Nyasa Love-bird.

Adult female: Similar to the male. Often appears larger and of a paler but brighter color.

Immature: Resembles the adult, except that the olive shade extends much further around the sides of the neck and down to the green mantle. Forehead slightly less richly colored.

This lovebird, formerly to all intents and purposes unknown to aviculture, was imported in 1926 in large numbers and is not a well-known aviary bird over a great part of the world. It seems to be a hardy and prolific species. The weather at the time was exceptionally bad, and when the young birds were nearly ready to fly, a raging blizzard covered the roof of the aviary with snow. A bitter hurricane blew for many days, during which it never stopped freezing and later there was a heavy fall of rain.

The nesting habits and requirements of Fischer's Lovebird resembles those of the Nyasa. It agrees fairly well with its own kind, though some pairs will kill their neighbor's young. A single bird I introduced into an aviary of finches proved exceedingly spiteful, quickly murdering two of its companions.

Hardy as it is in the ordinary way, Fischer's Lovebird will not thrive outdoors in winter if its nesting boxes are removed, even though it can be driven into the aviary shelter at night. It is necessary, therefore, to allow it to go on breeding. If the hen should get egg-bound, the shelter will need to be warmed. If, as is likely, few young are reared in the over-dry atmosphere of the shelter, the nests can be hung in the open flight where the rain will fall on them as soon as the warm nights return. Strange to say, though difficult to sex when adult, young birds just out of the nest show a decided difference in the size of the head and beak.

Young birds sometimes leave the nest fully fledged, but unable to fly. As no bird is more easily injured by a fall than a young lovebird it is prudent to lay a heap of fine resilient twigs beneath the entrance of the nest. The

The Fischer's Lovebird is not a shy species and can be quite a little bully towards other lovebird species if given the chance.

The Fischer's Lovebird is a hardy species that consumes a great deal of seeds and twigs in a day. All woodwork within the cage of one of these birds must be protected from its strong beak!

youngsters, when they emerge, should be picked up and put in a cage with clean blotting paper on the floor. Plenty of well-soaked millet and canary spray millet, crushed soaked hemp, shelled soaked sunflower, and stale brown bread crumbs should be sprinkled on the paper and renewed as they get dry or scratched into corners. Within 48 hours the young birds will begin to feed themselves if kept in a warm place. Care must be taken to provide both soaked millet and cracked hemp as some nestlings will sooner starve themselves than begin on millet and vice versa. As soon as the young birds are feeding well, the seed can be put in a dish and sand can replace the paper on the floor of the cage. After two weeks of

Blue Masked Lovebird. One of the earliest lovebird mutations to occur, the attractiveness of the coloration has ensured its popularity.

time, seed should be substituted for soaked because the soaked seed may make your birds obese. This initial wing weakness in the young is most common when the parents have a shortcoming or illness of some sort.

Fischer's Lovebirds should be fed on the same diet as Nyasas.

MASKED LOVE-BIRD—*AGAPORNIS PERSONATA*

Distribution: North-eastern Tanzania to Iringa Highlands

Adult male: Head blackish or blackish-brown merging into the yellow of the neck and upper breast, the latter sometimes tinged with orange on the throat. Remainder of plumage green, paler on the abdomen. Lower rump tinged with dull, dark blue. Tail marked with black. Bill red. Large white circles around the eye. Total length 5+ inches.

Adult female: Resembles the male. Often larger.

Immature: Slightly less richly colored than the adult.

This very striking looking lovebird has become one of the most common parrots on the bird market. It is among the hardiest of its tribe and among the most eager to go to nest. It is also, next to the Peach-face, the most spiteful. It will live well in an indoor or outdoor aviary, or in a flight cage, but it is cruel and

The Masked Lovebirds, along with the Peach-faced and the Fischer's Lovebirds are among the most popular and most numerous species in fanciers' aviaries.

stupid to confine it, or any other lovebird, in quarters so cramped that it cannot nest or freely use its wings.

The Masked Lovebird needs moisture in the nest for the successful development and hatching of the embryo chicks. For this reason the nest boxes should be hung in the open flight where rain can fall on them. My own females appear able to lay without trouble even in the coldest

Both sexes of the Masked Lovebird are alike, having a black mask that covers the entire head region. The throat and chest area is yellow with the rest of the body being green; the rump area is blue.

weather, but a friend of mine lost a hen from egg-binding, and if this ailment is feared, the only plan is to hang the nest boxes in a heated shelter during the cold months and risk poor hatching results until spring returns.

The Masked Lovebird lines its nest with fine twigs and strips of bark and continues to add material after the young have hatched, so the nest must be a big one or the young will be cramped.

The Masked Lovebird breeds continually, only stopping for the molt. Four eggs are the normal clutch, and the cock spends a good deal of time in the nest with his mate. The sexes are very hard to distinguish, but if you choose a specimen with a wide skull and one with a narrow one you will probably have a true pair. If you have not, you will soon be enlightened by the bird's behavior, for hens always go to nest without delay.

As already stated, the Masked Lovebird has a fiery temper, but unlike most pugnacious birds, it is not aroused to evil deeds by prosperity and intimidated by disturbance and misfortune, but vice versa. It is exceedingly risky to confine several adult birds in a cage or traveling box for they will surely injure each other due to living in close quarters. I had a bird torn to bits by its companions on a two hour journey. On the other hand one aviculturist has found the species tolerably well-behaved in mixed company when not interfered with, and my own two pairs, though they have had a couple of quarrels and removed the end of a few toes,

The Peach-faced Lovebird can be distinguished easily from other lovebird species by the pinkish-red head, neck, and throat area. The rump is a beautiful bright blue and the flight feathers are black.

have at least refrained from murdering each others' young in a 24ft x 8ft x 8ft aviary. On the whole, however, to prevent accidents and mutilation, I would certainly keep each pair alone.

The Masked Lovebird has the squeaking, chattering cries of its near relations, but is not disagreeably noisy.

It should be fed like the Nyasa Lovebird and is fond of oats softened by soaking. Hand-reared specimens make wonderful pets and prove to be very affectionate, alert and comical. A blue strain is a widely bred mutation in Europe and the US.

PEACH-FACED LOVEBIRD— *AGAPORNIS ROSEICOLLIS*

Distribution: South-western Africa

Adult male: Dull green, paler on the breast. Forehead bright rose-red; cheeks and throat rosy pink with a greyish tinge at the edge of the cheeks. Rump brilliant blue.

Tail short, blue green with black and fiery pink markings. Bill coral-red. Total length 6 inches.

Adult female: Resembles the male; usually, but not invariably, duller in color.

Immature: Has green areas of the plumage more brownish-olive. Forehead brownish; cheeks and throat brownish pink. Base of bill dark. Adult plumage is assumed within very few months.

Although, like all members of the lovebird family, the Peach-face is quite unsuited to life in a small cage; it will, if provided with a nest box to breed in and branches to nibble, readily adapt itself to life in any kind of aviary, birdroom, or even flight cage. There is, unfortunately, no absolutely certain way of distinguishing the sexes by their plumage. Since, however, the Peach-face belongs to that section of the lovebird family of which the main occupation is the reproduc-

Lovebirds are very active and their comical behavior is sure to provide great pleasure.

tion of its species on every possible occasion, an aviculturist need never remain long in doubt as to whether he possesses a true pair. If the birds are not molting, are in good condition and do not go to nest within a couple of months, they are males. If they both visit the nests and carry in building material on their backs, they are females. If only one carries building material and the other feeds it, they are a true pair. Peachfaces will make use of any kind of box or hollow log if it is sufficiently roomy to contain a good supply of fine strips of the bark of twigs of lime, elm, or poplar. Unlike some lovebirds their attempts at breeding are not easily rendered abortive by the fact that the nest is in a dry situation. The hen bird sits alone but the cock joins her in the nest at night, and may also enter it in times of emergency, especially when the young are very small and danger appears to threaten.

The Peach-face is an exceedingly spiteful bird, which will neither agree with its own kind, nor tolerate neighbors of other species, even those considerably larger than itself. It also has an annoying predisposition for biting toes. Sometimes the injury is inflicted in the ordinary course of combat with rivals, but in some cases it becomes an actual vice—parents maiming their young before they are independent and youngsters mutilating each other long before they are old enough to quarrel about mates or nesting places. There is no cure for this bad habit and birds addicted to it are best got rid of.

Some aviculturists have been successful in wintering the Peach-faced Lovebird in outdoor aviaries, but the writer has not found it completely hardy in very severe weather.

The species should be fed on canary, millet, and oats, as well as small amounts of hemp and sunflower; chickweed and other green food should be supplied to birds rearing young.

In addition to the chattering cries uttered by many members of the family, the Peach-face has a disagreeable penetrating shriek which has earned it a bad name with some aviculturists.

Although not every pair can be trusted to stay, Peach-faced Lovebirds can be bred at liberty during the summer months. Before being released they should be thoroughly accustomed to an aviary and to a nest box; they do not take at all readily to natural holes in trees. If, as one observer states, the Peach-face in its native land breeds in the nest of the sociable Weaverbird, this reluctance is easily explained.

The name "lovebird" was given to these little parrots because of the affection shown between paired birds. This affection is not, however, shown towards others, and severe fighting sometimes occurs instead.

Asiatic Parrots

ECLECTUS PARROT—*ECLECTUS RORATUS*

Distribution: New Guinea and many neighboring islands, North Queensland

Adult male: General plumage brilliant green; bend of wing, primary coverts, primary and secondary quills deep blue. Outer tail feathers deep blue. Under wing-coverts, auxiliaries, and a large patch on the side of the body bright red. Upper mandible coral with a yellowish tip; eyes brown. Total length 14 inches. Size somewhat larger than a Blue-fronted Amazon.

Adult female: General plumage bright red, inclining to crimson on the back, wings, and base of the tail. A band of blue across the mantel, a narrow circle of blue around the eye; abdomen and sides of the body purplish blue; bend of wing, primary coverts, outer portions of the primaries and tips of the secondaries deep blue. Tip of tail orange-red. Bill black.

The Eclectus Parrots have long been noted for the striking difference in the plumage of the sexes and some writers have mentioned them as a curious example of species where the female is more richly colored than the male.

Why a crimson bird should be considered more ornate then a brilliant green one is a little hard to understand.

When confined in parrot cages, Eclectus are usually very calm and very quiet pets. They quickly learn who their owner is and eagerly await

Eclectus Parrots are strikingly beautiful birds. The female is brilliant red in color while the male exhibits kelly green plumage.

attention from them. Once tame, they enjoy being petted and quickly learn to say a few words.

Of the Eclectus Parrot's voice, only one favorable thing can be said—-that he does not make very free use of it. Indeed, if he be at all dispirited and out of sorts he will not utter a sound of any kind. Let him be a little extra lively, however, or slightly alarmed, and the truly awful "Crrah!" is sounded. It goes through you like a knife, and I doubt if the whole realm of nature con-

tains another sound so incredibly harsh.

Eclectus Parrots should be fed like most other parrot-like birds. A good seed mixture containing sunflower and peanuts as well as other smaller seeds such as canary, millet and thistle. Fruit is a large part of their diet and should not be permitted to perish within the cage. They should not be kept in drafty quarters. They can not survive a winter outdoors in any but temperate climates with the proper amount of shelter. When in breeding condition they are of a somewhat savage and uncertain temper, especially with their own species.

Eclectus parrots are largely bred today in Europe and the United States and hybrids of nearly allied species have been reared in captivity. A hen Eclectus that laid in a cage was given a fowl's egg to sit on, which she hatched successfully. It is not recorded, however, how she got on with her active foster child!

My efforts to induce Eclectus Parrots to stay at liberty were completely unsuccessful. I did not, however, experiment with the male of a breeding pair whose mate was confined in an aviary.

The Blue-fronted Amazon reaches sexual maturity between the ages of three and five years. This handsome bird appears to be a hardy, mature specimen of the species.

BLUE-FRONTED AMAZON— *AMAZONA AESTIVA*

Distribution: Brazil, Paraguay, Argentina

Adult male: Green with faint bluish reflections on the fore-neck and breast. Feathers of hind-neck and mantle barred with black. Forehead pale blue; crown, cheeks and throat yellow. Bend of wing

Blue-fronted Amazon preening its feathers. The oil gland of all birds is located at the base of the back, near the rump. You will often see your Amazon using this gland to supply its feathers with oil to keep them looking shiny.

yellow mixed with red. Outer web of primaries bluish. Secondaries show a large patch of red; also blue and green coloring. Tail feathers green with terminal portion paler golden-green. A red patch near the base of the outer ones. Bill blackish. Length 14-15 inches.

Adult female: Resembles the male but has a narrower skull. The bend of the wing is usually red.

Immatures: The blue and yellow areas of the plumage are reduced in size.

The Blue-fronted Amazon is the best known bird of the Amazon species. The numbers of this bird even exceed those of the Grey Parrot. It takes well to cage life and usually makes an excellent talker and mimic. If not quite equal to the African bird in the number of words it can learn to repeat clearly, it surpasses its rival in its power of giving the general effect of a conversation, a song, or a person in tears; the mimicry being often exceedingly ludicrous. Some years ago my mother had a Pekingese dog of a very irascible disposition who particularly objected to the ministrations of the vet. A Blue-fronted Amazon we had at the time learned to give the most realistic representation of a stormy interview between Che Foo and his medical adviser, the infuriated yells of the dog mingling with the soothing words wherewith his friends endeavored to assuage his ill-humor.

The Blue-fronted Amazon has two short comings. Like all of its tribe it screams badly in moments of excitement and most, though not all, are liable to give an occasional nip even to their best friends, either when their jealousy is aroused by the presence of another parrot, or simply out of pure mischief. Covering the bird's cage as a punishment will sometimes teach it to control its desire to give vocal expression to its exuberant feelings, however, it is most often more effective if a deaf ear is turned.

Being very common and easy to obtain, there is no excuse for bad specimens. The advice given as to the general treatment of caged parrots is applicable to this Amazon. A nice sized cage that offers plenty of room for the bird to exercise without hitting its wings against the cage and a diet of seed mix and fruit will suffice. In order for your parrot to really thrive, however, a weekly bath and plenty of free time out of the cage is needed.

Blue-fronted Amazons are bred often in captivity and even the novice has had such success. The proper breeding accommodation would be a hollow tree-trunk, but a box or barrel partly filled with dried shavings will also serve. The female must not be allowed to lay when the nights are cold. Paired Blue-fronts, like Greys become excessively savage towards human owners during mating season.

In suitable climates Amazons can be wintered in an outdoor aviary. In adverse climates they sometimes suffer from pneumonia and enteritis. An Amazon attacked by the latter complaint often passes a quantity of blood, but with veterinary care this can be cured.

The Blue-fronted Amazon has been kept with success at liberty, though newly-released birds which have been long caged need watching in case they lose their bearings.

YELLOW-FRONTED AMAZON—*AMAZONA OCHROCEPHALA*

Distribution: Brazil, Ecuador, Venezuela, Trinidad, Eastern Peru

Adult: Green, paler on the head and yellower on the breast. Feathers of neck and mantle with dusky edges. Crown yellow. Flights blue and green with blackish webs. A red bar on the secondaries. A fiery-red patch near the base of the outer tail feathers. Bill blackish with flesh-colored base. About the size of the Blue-fronted, only slightly larger.

Immatures: Appear to lack the yellow on the crown and the red on the wing.

The Yellow-fronted Amazon makes an amusing talker and mimic. Dr. Butler mentions one that had entirely forgotten its own language and expressed all its emotions of rage, pleasure, fear, etc., as a child would, shouting and crying when startled or angry. It also appears to understand the meaning of some of the sentences it used. If anyone dressed for a walk appeared in the room the parrot would say: "Are you going out? Are you going to the park? There's a cat in the park. Good-bye!"

DOUBLE YELLOW HEAD AMAZON—*AMAZONA OCHROCEPHALA ORATRIX*

Distribution: Mexico, Yucatan, and Honduras

Adult: Green, paler and bluer on the breast. Head and neck golden yellow, paler on the crown. Mantle often flecked with yellow. Shoulder and bend of wing showing pinkish-red and yellow feathers. Wing-bar pinkish red, flights also showing blue,

A young Double Yellow Head Amazon. As the Double Yellow Head matures it obtains more yellow coloration to its head.

green and black coloring. Tail feathers have pale green tips; outer pair with a blue edging. A patch of fiery red near the base of the tail. Bill whitish. Iris red with inner ring yellow. Total length 15 inches. Size about that of the Blue-front.

The Double Yellow Head is thought to be the best talker of the genus. Its ability to mimic words, phrases, and songs surpasses most other Amazons.

Immatures: Show less yellow and have green on cheeks and crown.

The Double Yellow Head Amazon is a rather striking-looking parrot with its yellow head, white beak and red irises. It always gives the impression of being a color variety rather than the typical representative of a species. It is, perhaps, scarcely as hardy as the Blue-front, needing more room and exercise and the best of feeding with plenty of fruit. Individuals vary greatly in disposition, some being amiable, others fierce or treacherous. Though noisy, this species often proves to be a brilliant talker. Canon Dutton had one which sang seven songs, did the French military exercises, said other things and swore like a French sailor, and was always ready to perform at command. It was a gentle bird and bore its master no malice, though he had to hold it during a painful operation.

An old portrait by Marc Geerarts represents Lady Arabella Stuart with a Double Yellow Head Amazon, a Red and Green Macaw, and a pair of Red-faced Lovebirds. The date of the picture must be about 1590 and it is interesting to find that these birds were known to English aviculture at so early a date.

The female is said to be smaller and to have a shorter and broader beak.

PANAMA PARROT—*AMAZONA OCHROCEPHALA PANAMENSIS*

Distribution: Panama, Veraguas, Colombia

Adult: Green with faint bluish reflections on the crown, cheeks, throat and breast. A patch of yellow on the forepart of the crown. A patch of red at the shoulder. Outer webs of primaries dark blue. Secondaries show the usual red patch found in nearly all Amazons. Bill yellowish. Length 12-14 inches.

Immatures: Entire head green.

This sub-species is very difficult to distinguish from other *ochrocephala* species. Treatment as for the Yellow-shouldered.

YELLOW-NAPED AMAZON—*AMAZONA OCHROCEPHALA AUROPALLIATA*

Distribution: Western side of Central America

Adult: Green, paler on the breast and much paler on the head. Feathers of the sides of the neck and upper breast faintly barred with dusky

An excited Yellow-naped Amazon. When parrots of any species become excited or angered, they fluff their feathers, fan their tails, and pin their eyes.

color. Nape yellow; a few yellow feathers often present on the forehead. Flights green and blue with black inner webs, a pinkish red bar on the secondaries. Tail green with terminal half pale yellowish green. A patch of fiery red near the base of the outer tail feathers. Bill horn-grey with yellowish base. Total length 14 inches. About the size of the Blue-front. The male is often brighter and larger than the female with greater sheen to the feather.

The Yellow-naped Amazon is a somewhat rare bird in captivity, but very abundant in a wild state. An observer, writing in the year 1896, comments on the large numbers that came to roost in the vicinity of the houses of the town. It is known to make an excellent talker.

The female is said to have a narrower beak, more arched, and with a shorter terminal hook. The treatment should be that of the Blue-front.

The Yellow-naped Amazon is a very popular bird that is known for its affection, playfulness, and mimicry.

YELLOW-SHOULDERED AMAZON—*AMAZONA BARBADENSIS*

Distribution: Island of Aruba off Venezuela

Adult: Green with bright bluish reflections on the lower cheeks and breast. Crown, throat, and feathers below the eye golden yellow, orange-salmon at the base. Forehead frosted with white. Feathers of neck, mantle, and rump barred at the tip with black; the barring being most pronounced on the lower part of the back of the neck. Bend of the wing yellow, or yellow and red. Thighs yellow. Tail feathers green with pale tips, the outer ones showing a patch of wine color at the base. Flight feathers blue on the outer web, secondaries showing a large patch of red. Bill whitish-horn. Iris orange. Total length 13-14 inches. Wings about 8+ inches. Slightly smaller than the Blue-fronted Amazon.

Like all Amazon species, the Yellow-shouldered does much better in a large cage than in a smaller one that does not offer it much room. The food should be that of the Blue-fronted Amazon.

Old German aviculturists describe this parrot as very easily tamed but showing great individual variation in its powers of mimicry. Sounds were apt to be picked up more easily than words.

The female is said to have the region of the lower mandible, lower breast, and abdomen sky blue, and all the other colors duller than those of the male.

MEALY AMAZON—*AMAZONA FARINOSA*

Distribution: Guianas

Adult: Green, brighter on the cheeks. Neck, mantle, and rump show a mealy tinge. Feathers of back of crown and back of neck tipped with blackish color, the latter also

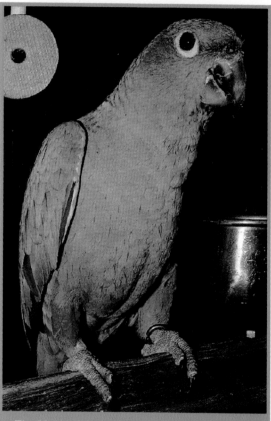

The Mealy Amazon is a large and gentle bird. It is larger than most Amazon species and therefore requires a slightly larger cage.

showing a bluish lilac tint towards the ends. A spot or patch of yellow, or yellow and scarlet, on the crown. Inner web of primaries black; secondaries showing an area of red, dark blue, and green. A little red at the bend of the wing. Tail green at the base; yellowish-green for the terminal half. Bill light horn color. Length 15 inches. Larger than the Blue-fronted Amazon.

The Mealy Amazon does somewhat better in an aviary than a cage and can be wintered out-of-doors. Its treatment should be that of the Blue-front.

This species proves to be extremely talented as well as gentle and friendly but unfortunately noisy.

MERCENARY AMAZON—*AMAZONA MERCENARIA*

Distribution: Peru, Ecuador, Bolivia

Adult male: Green, brighter on the cheeks and paler on the breast. Back of neck and mantle with a mealy tinge. Feathers of crown, neck, and upper mantle tipped with purplish black, the markings being heavy on the neck and faint elsewhere. Primaries with green bases and blackish webs. Secondaries showing a large patch of red, as well as dark blue. Bend of wing shows a few red and yellow feathers. Tail tipped with greenish yellow, outer feathers with a larger wine red patch in the middle. Bill dusky and yellowish near the base. Total length 13+ inches. Size about that of the Blue-front.

Immatures: Said to lack the red wing-bar.

FESTIVE AMAZON—*AMAZONA FESTIVA*

Distribution: Amazon Valley, up to Eastern Peru

Adult: Green, brighter and sometimes bluer on the cheeks and mealy on the back. A narrow line across the forehead, and feathers between eye and beak wine red. Tips of feathers above and behind the eye blue and a trace of blue on the crown. A

The Festive Amazon is not easily obtainable in the United States. It is a quieter Amazon than the other species, yet can mimic the human voice well.

trace of dark edging to the feathers of the neck. Upper rump crimson. Bastard wing dark blue. Outer edge of primaries dark blue. Secondaries green with a tinge of dark blue. Tail green. Outer

Green-cheeked Amazon displaying the bright red forehead and lores characteristic of the species.

feathers with the merest trace of wine red near the base of the quill. Bill dusky. Total length 14+ inches. Size about that of the Blue-front.

The Festive Amazon is a handsome parrot and has the reputation of being much less noisy than most of its allies. Individuals vary greatly in docility and talent, but the best are said to be brilliant talkers with very clear pronunciation.

Canon Dutton had a yellow specimen for a short time, but it does not seem certain that it was a pure lutino.

The female is said to have a shorter and fuller beak and to be smaller than the male.

The treatment is the same as for the Blue-front.

GREEN-CHEEKED AMAZON— *AMAZONA VIRIDIGENALIS*

Distribution: Eastern Mexico

Adult male: Green, very bright on the cheeks and paler on the breast. Cap and feathers in front of eye crimson. A strip of blue or lilac feathers extends over the area behind the eye. Feathers of hind-neck tipped with black. Primaries blue-black with faint pale tips. Secondaries with a large patch of red; also blue and green. Bill yellowish white, less short and curved than that of the Blue-fronted Amazon. Total length 13 inches. Size about that of the Blue-front.

Immatures: Said to have only the forehead and lores red, the crown being green.

The Green-cheeked Amazon is one of the most beautiful of the medium-sized Amazons. It does well in captivity but is somewhat rare and there appears to be little recorded of its character and habits. It should be fed like the Blue-fronted Amazon.

The female is said to have less red on the crown and a smaller beak.

SPECTACLED AMAZON— *AMAZONA ALBIFRONS*

Distribution: Western Mexico, Yucatan, Guatemala, Nicaragua, and Costa Rica

Adult: Green, brighter on the cheeks and breast and faintly barred with black on the neck. Forepart of crown white; rear part blue. Feathers around and eye and beak red. Some bright red on the lower edge of the wing. Flight feathers rich dark blue and green with blackish inner webs. A patch of wine red near the base of the outer tail feathers. Bill light yellow. Total length 10+ inches. Much smaller than the Blue-front.

Female has less white on the crown, and is smaller and duller than the male.

Immatures: Have less red on the wing, and probably less white and more blue on the crown.

This very small and rather striking-looking Amazon is steadily increasing in its numbers in captivity. It does poorly in a small parrot cage, but will live well in a flight cage suited for a larger parrot. Little is known of its ability to stand cold and it would be unwise to expose it to a low temperature without great caution. The food should be the same as for the Blue-fronted Amazon.

LILAC-CROWNED AMAZON—*AMAZONA FINSCHI*

Distribution: Western Mexico

Adult male: General plumage green, paler and more yellowish on underparts and brighter green on cheeks. Forehead and arc between eye and beak dull red. Crown and outer edge of cheeks lilac with a few green feathers interspersed. Feathers of neck and breast edged with black. A pinkish red bar on the wing, with the flights showing blue and green areas. Outer tail feathers have paler tips and a yellowish patch on the inner webs. Bill dirty white. Total length 13 inches. A little smaller than the Blue-fronted Amazon.

In its wild state this parrot is said to fly in large flocks and to be very active and graceful on the wing.

The female is said to have a broader and shorter beak, and is smaller and duller than the male.

The Lilac-crowned Amazon is named so for the patch of lilac on the top of the head and extending down to the nape.

BLACK-BILLED AMAZON—*AMAZONA AGILIS*

Distribution: Jamaica

Adult: Green, darker on the crown and paler on the breast. A scarlet patch on the lower edge of the wing. Flights blue and green, with black inner webs. Bill greyish-black. Total length 10+ inches. Much smaller than the Blue-front.

Immatures: Have no red in the wings and the flights are a duller blue.

The female is said to have a shorter and broader beak with a shorter terminal hook.

YELLOW-BILLED AMAZON—*AMAZONA COLLARIA*

Distribution: Jamaica

Adult: Green, very bright on the breast and yellowish on the tail coverts. Forehead white; more rarely pink. Crown dark bluish with black edgings to the feathers. Feathers of the neck edged with black and a trace of the same marking on the mantle. Throat deep pink. Outer web of flight feathers slate blue. Tail yellowish green, outer feathers with a deep pink patch near the base. Bill whitish. Length about 12 inches. Smaller than the Blue-front.

The Yellow-billed or Jamaican Amazon is not very common in captivity. It has the reputation of being affectionate, but noisy and a poor talker. Like most of the smaller Amazons it needs more exercise than permanent confinement that a parrot cage permits. It should be fed like the Blue-front.

YELLOW-LORED AMAZON—*AMAZONA ALBITRONS XANTHOLORA*

Distribution: Yucatan, Cozumel Island, British Honduras

Adult: Dark green, paler and yellower on the tail-coverts. Feathers edged with black most heavily on the neck, mantle, and upper breast. Forepart of crown white with rear edge dark blue. Feathers above, below, and at the back of eye bright red. Feathers between beak and eye and a small spot under the lower mandible are yellow. Flights green and dark blue with blackish inner webs A patch of scarlet on the lower edge of the wing. A patch of wine red near the base of the outer tail feathers. Bill yellow. Total length 10+ inches. Much smaller than the Blue-fronted Amazon.

Immatures: Appear to have the crown mainly blue and less red around the eye and on the wing.

This curious little Amazon is extremely rare in captivity. It is actually a local race of the Spectacled Amazon and should be treated in the same way. It requires more care than its larger relatives.

CUBAN AMAZON—*AMAZONA LEUCOCEPHALA*

Distribution: Cuba, Island of Pines

Adult: Green, yellowish on the tail coverts. Forehead white, sometimes tinged with rose. Cheeks and an irregular patch on the throat rose red or rose pink. Feathers of the forepart of the body edged with black, the markings being heaviest on the head and neck. Feathers of abdomen show a considerable amount of wine color. Outer web of flights slate blue. Tail yellowish green, outer feathers with a large red or wine red patch near the base. Bill whitish. Total length 12-13 inches. Slightly smaller than the Blue-front.

The Cuban is the most frequently imported of the group of dark green Amazons with pink or white on the face and throat. It is a very beautiful bird but is noisy and an indifferent

talker and does better in an aviary, birdroom, or flight cage than in very close confinement.

This Amazon is not particularly reliable at liberty, but I once had a female which spent the winter free in the garden and paired with a young male Adelaide Parakeet. Strange to say the latter was bred at liberty and had never known confinement and it is extraordinary that at less than 12 months old he should have deserted the company of his own kind for that of the parrot. When spring came around the Adelaide was most attentive in feeding his strange partner and the pair set up house in a hollow oak, but just when the breeding of remarkable hybrids seemed possible the Amazon unfortunately died.

A breeding pair of Cuban Amazons in their wild habitat.

RED-MASKED CONURE— *ARATINGA ERYTHROGENYS*

Distribution: West Ecuador

Adult: Green. Crown and face red. Some spots of red on the neck. Shoulders, under wing-coverts, thighs, and bend of wing red. Bill yellowish white. Length 13+ inches.

Immatures: Much less red.

The Red-masked Conure is a typical member of a larger group of South American parakeets which have a strong family resemblance in character and habits. They make affectionate, intelligent, and playful pets, but are too active to be suited to permanent confinement in a parrot cage. If caged they must be let out daily for exercise and permitted to chew up wood and other relatively soft substances. Most species are hardy and can be wintered in

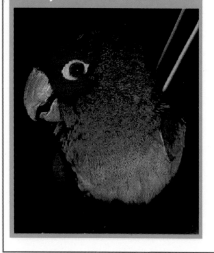

Red-masked Conure. This is a very popular conure species that, like most of the conure family, has the unfortunate shortcoming of being rather noisy.

outdoor aviaries. The chief fault of the genus is their excessive noisiness and spitefulness towards parakeets of other families. Like lorikeets they are a little less tolerant of their own kind and of non-psittacine birds.

They nest fairly freely in captivity and are usually double brooded. In their domestic arrangements, they

Conures are very friendly birds that train easily and prove to be very affectionate.

closely resemble lorikeets, and they will use a hollow log or tree trunk in aviary shelter or flight.

They appreciate logs to roost in, but a careful watch must be kept in case a hen tries to lay in cold weather and gets egg-bound. Where this danger has arisen, the log must be put in a heated shelter and the birds driven in

at night. It may be added that it is a great mistake to leave nests in the aviary out of the breeding season where species are kept which do *not* use them as dormitories. Conures should be fed on a seed mixture of two parts canary, one part millet, one part oats, and one part peanuts with plenty of fruit. Too much hemp is liable to cause liver disease and feather plucking. The sexes are always very much alike.

The Red-masked Conure makes a fair talker.

GREEN CONURE—*ARATINGA HOLOCHLORA*

Distribution: Guiana, Trinidad, Colombia, Peru, Bolivia, Brazil

Adult male: Green. Sometimes with speck of red on the head or neck, or a tinge of wine red on the breast. Bend of wing and under wing-coverts orange-red, the latter merging into yellow. Bill yellowish flesh-color. Naked skin around eye, ashy flesh-color. Length 13+ inches.

Immatures: Bend of wing yellowish.

A rarely imported species, which, like other large conures, atones for its harsh voice and not particularly beautiful plumage by unusual intelligence and docility and talent for talking.

The female is said to have a broader beak.

GOLDEN CONURE—*ARATINGA GUAROUBA*

Distribution: Para, Northeast Brazil

Adult male: General plumage rich golden yellow, flight feathers dark green. Bill pinkish horn; feet flesh color. Total length 14 inches.

Adult female: Similar to the male but smaller and with a less massive head and beak.

Immatures: Nestling plumage shows more green. At a certain stage has cheeks and upper wing-coverts with scattered green feathers.

The Golden Conure, also known as Queen of Bavaria's Conure, has long been famous for its great rarity; its docility when tamed, and its marvelous golden plumage. I have had a strong interest in conures, and the Queen of Bavaira was a most welcome addition to my collection. Certainly though not graceful in form, and endowed with a voice as disagreeable as that of any of his noisy congeners, the Golden Conure has a barbaric splendor that cannot fail to attract.

Although my none in my collection of this species are tame, I can well believe that the accounts of their good

Fanciers of the Golden Conure often call it the most intelligent member of its genus.

qualities as pets are not over-rated, for they are continually caressing each other, and playing together in the most amusing fashion, shoving and mauling like puppies, yet never evoking a protest by too hard a nip. They are typical conures in all their habits, ruffling their feathers, doing all kinds of gymnastics and assaulting any parakeet of another family that approaches them, for although single birds are harmless enough in mixed company, pairs are decidedly aggressive.

The Golden Conure is not easy to obtain. If you are lucky enough to purchase one of these birds know that they are extremely playful and love attention.

Unfortunately, no parakeet in existence is more addicted to the vice of feather plucking than the Golden Conure. Even the plainest diet combined with plenty of exercise in a large outdoor aviary and a companion of the opposite sex will not prevent some birds from disfiguring themselves.

The Golden Conure should be fed on sunflower and canary seed with an unlimited supply of apple and other fruit.

When tamed, the species is said to make a good talker.

PEACH-FRONTED CONURE—ARATINGA AUREA

Distribution: Guiana, Amazons, Bolivia, Paraguay

Adult: Green, forepart of crown and feathers around the eye orange-salmon. Rear of crown bluish. Throat, cheeks, and upper breast olive, the cheeks have a faint bluish tinge. Lower breast pale yellowish green. Flights blue green. Tail tip tinged with blue. Bill blackish. Total length 10+ inches.

The Peach-fronted Conure has been bred many times in captivity. The species is easily tamed and becomes docile and affectionate, but breeding pairs are spiteful with other birds.

The female of this species is said to have a shorter and broader beak, but this is not necessarily so.

PATAGONIAN CONURE—CYANOLISEUS PATAGONUS

Distribution: La Plata and Patagonia

Adult: Dark, brownish olive, paler and more bronze on the wing, and less olive on the upper breast. A little whitish color on the upper breast. Abdomen yellow with a large orange-red patch on the center. Rump pale golden-bronze. Flights slate color. Bill horn black. Length 17+ inches.

The Patagonian Conure, though not a gaudy bird, is decidedly handsome in its unusual garb of brown and

The Patagonian Conure is the largest of the conures, measuring between 17-20 inches in length.

yellow. Like other big conures it is very intelligent, a good talker and mimic, and an amusing and playful companion.

The species is quite indifferent to cold, and, it breeds in colonies in burrows in the face of cliffs, is probably tolerant of the presence of other conures.

The female is said to be smaller, with a smaller, shorter and broader beak.

ORANGE-FRONTED CONURE—*ARATINGA CANICULARIS*

Distribution: Mexico and Central America

Adult: Glittering olive green. Abdomen bright yellow-green. Throat and upper breast pale yellowish olive brown. Forepart of crown salmon color. Rear of crown slate blue. Flights blue-green. Bill fleshy-white. Length 9+ inches.

Immatures: Much less salmon on the forehead.

This little conure makes a nice pet.

In the wild state it feeds largely on the fruit of the tree *Pileus conica* and soils its plumage badly with the sticky juice. This circumstance is not a little remarkable when one recollects how strongly healthy birds object, as a rule, to dirt on their feathers; but I have seen skins of wild Amazon parrots badly disfigured from the same cause.

It is said that the Orange-fronted Conure is difficult to distinguish from the fruit on which it feasts so greedily and is apparently aware of the protective resemblance, as it remains quiet and motionless when a hawk surprises it on a "Parrot fruit" tree, but takes to noisy flight if approached by its enemy elsewhere.

AZTEC CONURE—*ARATINGA NANA ASTEC*

Distribution: Southern Mexico, Guatemala, Honduras, Nicaragua, and Costa Rica

Adult: Green. Throat and upper breast brown. Lower breast yellowish olive brown. Flights tinged with bluish slate. Bill brown-horn color. Length 9+ inches.

The Aztec Conure is breeds well in a flight cage, and as with most small conures, more than one brood is produced in a year. The normal clutch consists of four or five eggs. The female is said to have a broader beak.

CUBAN CONURE—*ARATINGA EUOPS*

Distribution: Cuba

Adult male: Green. Cheeks, crown and bend of wing flecked with scarlet. Under wing-coverts scarlet. Bill whitish flesh-color. Length 10+ inches.

A rarely-imported bird, said to be intelligent and amusing.

BROWN-THROATED CONURE—*ARATINGA PERTINAZ OCULARIS*

Distribution: Veraguas and Panama

Adult: Green, paler and yellower on the breast. Crown slightly tinged with bluish slate color. Cheeks, throat and upper breast brown. Some orange feathers below the eye and sometimes a slight tinge of orange on the abdomen. Bill horn-brown. Length 9+ inches.

The Brown-throated Conure is not a timid bird and enjoys human companionship. In their native habitat they are often found nesting in trees closest to homes of the natives.

The Brown-throated Conure was bred in captivity and found to be quiet with non-psittacine birds and not destructive to shrubs. If teased, the pair performed very quaint antics, but did not bite. Nesting operations lasted nine weeks.

CACTUS CONURE—*ARATINGA CACTORUM*

Distribution: Southeastern Brazil

Adult: Green. Head tinged with brown and faint slate color. Flights and tip of tail tinged with slate blue. Throat and upper breast brown. Lower breast yellowish buff. Bill whitish. Length 10+ inches.

Immatures: Crown plain green. Throat and breast olive.

This rather pretty little conure does well in confinement and has been wintered out-of-doors. It has the family failing of noisiness, but is said to agree fairly well with other members of the genus. It becomes very tame and amusing, single birds, and even pairs, showing a lively interest in their owner, run-

Sun Conures have proven to be the most prolific members of the genus *Aratinga*.

ning to meet him fluttering and jabbering in a sort of ecstasy. The species breeds well in captivity. Treatment as for other conures.

The female is said to be smaller and to have a shorter beak.

JENDAYA CONURE—*ARATINGA JANDAYA*

Distribution: Brazil

Adult: Head and neck orange-yellow. Breast and under wing-coverts orange-red tinged with olive. Thighs olive and tinged with rust red. Upper rump orange-red; lower rump green. Mantle and wings green: lower edge of

Nanday Conures are very playful and affectionate towards their owners. They do, however, have the typical shortcoming of a loud voice as other members of their family.

wing and flights partly blue. Tail bronze-green at the top. Bill dusky horn color. Length 12 inches.

The Jendaya is a common species that does well in an aviary and is reputed to be peaceable with other birds. It breeds well in captivity, nesting operations taking about three months from start to finish. The species has

some talent for mimicry, but the usual conure failing of a harsh voice and a mischievous beak.

NANDAY CONURE— *NANDAYUS NENDAY*

Distribution: Paraguay

Adult: Bright green. Crown brownish black merging into chestnut at the rear edge. Front of cheeks marked with black or black and chestnut. A pale bluish tinge on the upper breast. Thighs rust red. Flights, lower edge of wing, and tail blue and green. Bill horn-brown. Length 12 inches. Female with a smaller head and more sharply curved beak.

Immatures: Duller.

This rather handsome conure is well-known in captivity and breeds frequently. It is noisy, but can be wintered out-of-doors and is said to agree fairly well with other members of the conure family. Food and treatment as for other conures.

THICK-BILLED PARROT— *RHYNCHOPSITTA PACHYRHYNCHA*

Distribution: Mexico

Adult: Green, brighter on the cheeks. Forepart of crown, feathers above and behind eye, shoulders, and a touch on the thighs and lower edge of the wing, red. Lower part of under-coverts yellow. Bill black. Length 17 inches.

Immatures: Less red; bill horn-whitish.

This large conure-like parakeet is extremely rare in captivity. The species has some virtues to offset its harsh voice and powerful beak, a tame bird in my collection shows great affection for me and follows me about with a queer shuffling gait, shaking its tail from side to side.

The species would no doubt thrive on the treatment of a conure.

MONK PARAKEET—*MYIOPSITTA MONACHUS*

Distribution: Bolivia, Paraguay, Argentine, Uruguay

Adult male: Green, brighter on the rump and belly. Forehead and lower part of cheeks grey with pale edges to the feathers; lower breast greyish olive. Flights and bastard-wing bluish. Tail long and narrow, green slightly tinged with blue. Bill reddish white. Total length 11+ inches. Size about that of a Ringneck.

Adult female said to be more bulky and with a much longer and more powerful beak.

The Monk Parakeet has the distinction of being the only parrot which is known to build an actual nest. It is an excessively hardy bird and the only thing that will kill it is permanent confinement in a parrot cage. It is highly gregarious in a wild state, even during the breeding season. The old nests are repaired and re-occupied until they reach a great size. When not employed for the rearing of a brood they are kept in good condition for a dormitory. A species of Teal, *B. monachus*, often lays its eggs in the Monks's nests and appears to live on quite good terms with the rightful own-

ers. The nest itself is entirely composed of sticks and consists of two chambers, an inner and an outer one. As the young brood increases in size the parents sometimes reconstruct and enlarge the nursery. From four to six eggs are usually laid and the period of incubation is 31 days.

The Monk is a noisy bird, continually uttering its "Quak, quaki, quak-wi, quak-wi, quak-wi, quarr! Guarr!

All parrots, at one time or another, will "test" their owners. They begin to get a little aggressive and try to ignore what it is that you wish them to do. This Monk Parakeet does not want to get off its owner's shoulder.

Quarr!" Some people find its vocal efforts distressing, but in justice it must be admitted that while the Monk talks far, far too much, he just fails to reach the unendurable pitch in all his remarks. Pet birds are intelligent and amusing. An aviculturist had one which was an excellent talker, its longest sentence being "Merrily danced the Quaker's wife with all her brains about her." It would do tricks to order. At the command "Act draft!" it would ruffle its feathers, put up one leg, open its beak, and nod its head. At the com-

mand "Act proud!" it would turn its beak against its breast and draw up its head. It showed great affection for its owners, but would attack visitors and strange dogs and cats and pull off ladies' hats. It was never caged during the day. It bathed freely and was so indifferent to cold that it would dry itself on the crack between two window sashes through which a keen north-easter was blowing.

The Monk Parakeet will flourish in an outdoor aviary and not be bothered by the cold. It requires a strong gauge wire housing, as it can bite through ordinary wire.

For breeding, a larger heap of twigs and sticks must be provided and a framework or platform as a foundation for the nest. Both sexes share in the work of building. The Monk Parakeet agrees well with its own kind but is very savage with all other birds, a pair delivering a joint attack after the manner of lorikeets.

The Monk Parakeet should be fed on canary, millet, oats, and sunflower with peanuts and plenty of fruit. The species breeds well in captivity in Europe and in the United States. The Monk Parakeet cannot be considered an ideal aviary subject for if it should escape to the wild it will destroy gardens, orchards, crops, etc. by sheering off innumerable branches and committing havoc.

Cockatoos and Cockatiel

PALM COCKATOO—
PROBOSCIGER ATERRIMUS

Distribution: Papuan Islands and North Australia

Description: Black, the races from the New Guinea region have a slate grey tinge. A patch of naked pink skin exists at the base of the beak. Bill of great size and black in color. Upper mandible notched. Eye large and dark. A long crest of hair-like feathers. Total length 29 inches.

Adult female: Smaller and more slender, with a much smaller head and beak.

This extraordinary-looking cockatoo was rare in aviculture until recent years, when a number-mostly males-were imported, both the New Guinea race and the smaller subspecies being represented. Today it is highly bred in captivity.

The Palm Cockatoo was once a rare species to find in captivity. Today, due to conscious efforts by breeders, the Palm is becoming more prolific in homes and aviaries in the United States.

In the wild state the Palm Cockatoo is said to subsist on nuts and on the green center of the palm cabbage. Its eggs are laid in a hollow tree on a bed of green twigs.

In captivity it has the reputation of being a very gentle bird, not biting even when annoyed but merely scratching with the tip of its upper mandible. It enjoys being petted and is known to have a small vocabulary. The curious bare pink skin on the face is capable of changing color and becomes bluish when the bird is cold or ill.

The Palm Cockatoo's natural call consists of whistles, screams, and croaks, and when hurt or terrified it utters a loud grating screech.

Palm Cockatoos should be fed on hemp, sunflower, peanuts, and any other nuts or grain that they fancy. They will sometimes also eat apple and green food and softfood should be offered to birds with young.

The courtship of the Palm Cockatoo is the quaintest and most ludicrous of any member of the parrot family and perhaps of any bird in the world. Blushing bright red with excitement, the male erects his weird crest, spreads his wings, stamps his feet, and utters the most incredible assortment of whoops, shrieks and strange clicking noises. At frequent intervals he ducks his head sharply and turns it on one side gazing adoringly up into the face of his beloved.

Male Palm Cockatoos feed their mates but do not caress them and take no part in the incubation of the eggs. A large natural tree trunk makes the best nest and the birds should be plentifully supplied with leafy branches as they are said to line their nests profusely, no doubt as a precaution against their being filled by tropical rain.

RED-TAILED COCKATOO—
CALYPTORHYNCUS MAGNIFICUS

Distribution: Australia

Adult male: Black with a dull gloss on the wings and a faint greyish tinge on the breast. A long scarlet bar across the outer tail feathers. Bill greyish black. Length 27 inches.

Adult female: Black, feathers of head, neck, and mantle with dull, pale yellow spots. Breast barred with dull, pale yellow. Under tail-coverts pale yellow and orange-red with black bars and freckling. Tip of tail black; basal portion pale yellow merging into orange-red with transverse black bars and black specking.

Immatures: In first plumage much resembles the female. With the first molt young males become less spotted and show more red on the tail than females of the same age. With the second molt they become entirely black with scarlet tail bars specked with black. With the third, adult plumage is assumed.

Red-tailed Cockatoos in flight. The sexes of this species can be distinguished readily by the differently colored tail bands. This marking has a significant function not only in courtship; in flight it ensures that the flock keep together.

The Red-tailed Cockatoo is a variable species of which three or four races exist, differing considerably in size and to some extent in the plumage of the females and the dimension of the beak.

The typical Red-tail is a big race. The female has the head well-spotted and the breast well-barred, the tail feathers show pale yellow and orange-red color. The voice of the male when in flight is deep, melancholy, and sonorous.

The Great-billed Red-tailed Cockatoo is about as large as the typical form, but has a larger beak, while the female has scarcely any orange-red in her tail—pale yellow coloring predominating. The Western Red-tailed Black Cockatoo is about a third smaller than the two forms already mentioned. The voice of the male is pitched in a higher key and the female is very profusely spotted and barred, her tail being like that of the nominate race in coloring.

In a wild state the Red-tailed Cockatoo occurs in fairly large flocks, although it seems to be diminishing under persecution for its feathers and flesh, as well as with the settlement of the country. A party of Red-tails have a habit, not uncommon among parrots, of refusing to leave a wounded companion, their concern exposing them to still further casualties from a person armed with a gun.

In their nesting habits they resemble the broadtailed parakeets, and differ from most other cockatoos, the male feeding his sitting mate, but making no attempt to incubate the eggs. The normal clutch consists of two, but single eggs are common.

Red-tailed Cockatoos are seldom seen in captivity and command very high prices. Presumably the nests are inaccessible and the young troublesome to rear, while adults usually refuse food and die when deprived of their liberty. Birds accustomed to

eating seed are, however, as easy to keep as their more common white brethren and will survive for a long period either in cage or aviary. A female in my collection must have been at least 20 years in captivity and is still a magnificent specimen showing not a sign of age.

By reason of their great size, their powerful beaks, and their loud and strident cries, Red-tails are certainly not everybody's birds, but they have a dignity and charm about them which endears them to the aviculturist who has proper accommodation to place at their disposal. The males become exceedingly tame; so tame, in fact, that it is almost impossible to find one that is of any use for breeding; their affections and interest become so centered in humanity that they have no time for the females of their own kind. No animal will give his master a more disinterested devotion than a Red-tailed Cockatoo. Unlike most cockatoos they dislike being touched and having their heads scratched, and at most tolerate rather than enjoy such familiarities; they have also little fondness for tidbits. All that they ask is to be with their master or mistress, a few kind words and a little flattery will evoke from them a transport of excitement and delight. They throw up their crests into the shape of a Roman helmet, spread their tails and go off into their peculiar love-song, "Kooi, kooi, kooi, kooi." A very tame male who lived for but a short two years in my collection, was one of the most interesting and delightful birds I have ever kept. With little difficulty

A beautiful pair of Gang Gang Cockatoos. Note the brighter plumage of the male.

pleasant companion in a room. As an aviary bird it is one of the most desirable of the cockatoos, for, though it is less beautifully colored than the Leadbeater and Salmon-crest, it is irresistibly quaint and amusing. The red-headed male and his grey mate in my possession are most comical. They are much attached to each other and indulge in a continual flow of small talk in a minor key, which occasionally develops into a duet of a more audible and by no means harmonious description. When on the wing they continually utter a loud screeching "Ky-or-ark!" Their flight bears a very close resemblance to that of the Short-eared Owl. They have the same long, round tipped wings, the same method of alighting and the same complete noiselessness. When acclimatized they are indiffer-

ent to cold and will breed readily in a suitable aviary. Both sexes incubate the eggs, the male sitting on the eggs quite as much as his partner. When rearing young, they should be supplied with a great deal of softfood.

Toward other cockatoos the Gang-gang is rather savage and aggressive, particularly when kept in pairs.

The food should consist of a well balanced parrot seed mixture. Like most cockatoos, they too are fond of apple. The species is very prone to feather plucking and a constant supply of branches must be kept in the aviary for the birds to bite up the entire day.

The Gang-gang Cockatoo does well at liberty, and a pair will often stay and nest in the vicinity of their owner's home if care is taken to allow the male to be loose for several months before his mate is permitted to join him. If an additional precaution is desired, the male and female can be let out alternately, each for some months at a time, before they are allowed their freedom together. Gang-gangs roam to some distance from their feeding place. Consequently, it is inadvisable to keep this species at liberty when you have neighbors close by who are particular about their ornamental

shrubbery or about their garden and fruit trees.

WHITE-TAILED BLACK COCKATOO— *CALYPTORHYNCHUS FUNEREUS BAUDINII*

Distribution: Southwestern Australia

Adult: Brownish black, feathers tipped with pale buff. A whitish patch in the region of the ear. An incomplete white bar across the tail. Bill lead color. Length 23 inches.

Young birds of this species were imported by Mr. Frostick many years ago, and fed by hand on sponge cake and hard-boiled egg. He had difficulty in inducing them to take to seed and they unfortunately succumbed to fits no doubt by reason of the too-stimulating properties of the egg. He describes them as charmingly tame and intelligent, but tremendous wood biters even at an early age. Possibly, sterner measures would have forced the birds to adopt a more wholesome diet. The Black Cockatoos have tremendous powers of fasting and a hunger-strike of a few days does them no harm whatsoever.

GALAH COCKATOO (ROSE BREASTED)—*EOLOPHUS ROSEICAPILLUS*

Distribution: Widely distributed over the interior of the Australian Continent

Adult male: Back, wings, and tail grey, paler on the lower back, rump, and upper tail-coverts. Flight feathers darker grey; crown of head and hind neck pinkish white; throat, sides of face, breast, abdomen, and under wing-coverts rich rose-pink, deepening considerably, without a

The crest of the Galah Cockatoo is short when erected. Cockatoos only erect their crests when they become excited or aggressive.

molt, at the approach of the breeding season. Feet and legs mealy black. Bill greyish white. Iris so dark in color as to appear black. Length 14+ inches. Both sexes have a short erectile crest.

Adult female: Similar to the male but slightly more slender in build. Iris hazel or reddish, providing an easy indication of sex.

Immatures: In first plumage have the pink of the breast paler and considerably tinged with grey. Adult plumage is assumed with the first complete molt which begins in the spring following the year of their birth. I am inclined to think that the sexual distinction in the color of the eye is slight or absent in birds under a year old.

The Galah Cockatoo is exceedingly abundant in its native land and is also the best known member of its genus in Europe.

Many writers have described the beauty of a large flock of "Galahs" in a wild state. "Usually when the weather is broken and unsettled, though, often on a windy winter morning, or in thundery weather in March or April, against the grey masses of cloud which bank up, forming a somber background, it would seem as if all the Galahs in the vicinity had gathered in one flock, shrieking and screaming as they circled high in the air, all beating their wings in perfect unison. So, as it were at a given signal, the delicate rose-colored breasts are all turned one way, making a beautiful glow of color as the birds veer around; then, with one beat the flock seems almost to have disappeared, just a glimpse of silvery grey flashing as they turn their backs; then a mere speck where each bird is flying, so small that one would hardly believe it to be a bird, so almost invisible does the grey become; then a flash of silvery light before the glow of their breasts flashes into view again."

From the avicultural point of view the Galah Cockatoo possesses a good many virtues and some failings. As a talker it has seldom much merit, though a hand-reared bird may learn to say a few words. Like most cockatoos, it can, when excited, yell distractingly and if

kept in an aviary, woodwork will not survive the attacks of its beak. On the other hand, it is easily tamed and becomes devotedly attached to its owner. It is intelligent and playful, and, although one cannot help feeling some regret at keeping it in close confinement, it will take quite kindly to cage life.

The Galah Cockatoo should be fed on a well balanced parrot mixture containing many smaller seeds as well. Raw carrot or any kind of wholesome green food may be offered and a fresh turf of grass is usually much appreciated. Fruit may be given, but is seldom much relished. A small log of wood, preferably with the bark on, will provide the bird with much amusement and exercise for its beak. On no account should a Galah Cockatoo or any other

When the crest of the Galah is not erect it is difficult to see.

GREATER SULPHUR–CRESTED COCKATOO—*CACATUA GALERITA*

Distribution: Widely distributed over Australia

Adult male: White, with sulphur yellow crest, under surface of tail, and inner webs of primary and secondary quills. Bill black. Iris almost black. Total length 20 inches.

Adult female: Resembles the male, but is said to have a slightly paler iris, though this is doubtful.

Immatures: Said to resemble the adults.

The Sulphur–crested Cockatoo is a very common bird in Australia, congregating in large flocks and laying its two white eggs, either in hollow trees or in holes in the face of a cliff. One observer writes, "They are found all year along the (Murray) river and a great distance back. They congregate in great numbers at nesting time and take possession of the holes worn by the weather into the high cliffs, rising several hundreds of feet out of the water; here they lay their eggs

Aside from being beautiful the Greater Sulphur-crested Cockatoo is naturally a tame and affectionate species. Birds of this species thrive with human companionship.

A performing Greater Sulphur-crested Cockatoo rides a bicycle along a tightrope. Cockatoos are very talented birds that are able to learn tricks easily.

upon the bare sand and hatching out their young. It is a very interesting sight to see many hundreds of these birds half out of their nesting holes or sitting upon the ledge of rocks near their nests; depressing and raising their beautiful yellow crests. They are very noisy birds and keep up a continual screeching call."

The Sulphur–crested Cockatoo is very destructive to growing crops and is much hated by the farmers, who kill them wholescale either by scattering poisoned grain, or by putting poison into drinking places. While appreciating the point of view of the settlers whose livelihood is threatened, this terribly cruel method of destruction is

much to be regretted, as not only are the chief offenders killed, but numbers of rare, beautiful, and sometimes harmless birds perish with them. It is particularly hard that the Australian authorities should ban the export of these birds, even under humane conditions and for the purposes of legitimate aviculture, when every year thousands are poisoned and the bodies left to rot on the ground.

As a cage bird the Sulphur–crested Cockatoo is hardy and enduring and there are records of individuals living to a stupendous age—over 100 years in a few cases. The bird becomes very tame and much attached to its owner, sometimes allowing even strangers to handle it with impunity. It also makes a fair talker, but, like all its tribe, is given in moments of excitement to yelling in the most appalling fashion.

The Sulphur–crest is perfectly hardy in an outdoor aviary, however, thought needs to be used in building. The strongest material must be used to resist its powerful beak. When suitably housed it is quite ready to go to nest. I am a little uncertain as to whether the color of the iris is a reliable guide as to sex in the species. Mr. Whitley, who owns a breeding pair, informs me that this hen has a slightly paler eye than her mate, but I have only once seen a Sulphur–crest with an eye that did not look black, so if the light iris is always characteristic of the female, the number of hens must be exceedingly small.

In disposition the Sulphur–crest is inclined to be somewhat aggressive to other parrot–like birds of large size.

At liberty this species has been kept with some measure of success and young have been reared. Although a handsome and imposing bird on the wing it is decidedly destructive to trees and is inclined to range some distance from home. Cock and hen should be released alternately for some months before they are allowed free together.

The Sulphur–crested Cockatoo should be given a well balanced parrot seed mixture containing canary, oats, hemp, sunflower, and peanuts, as well as any raw vegetables it will eat. Fruit may be offered, and is usually greatly relished. This cockatoo must have made its first

appearance in England a surprisingly long time ago, as a portrait by Simon Verelot, painted about the middle of the 17th century, shows a little girl with a pet bird unmistakably belonging to this species.

BLUE–EYED COCKATOO— *CACATUA OPHTHALMICA*

Distribution: New Britain

Adult: White. Part of crest lemon yellow. A faint yellow tinge on the inner webs of some of the flights and tail feathers. Naked skin around eyes blue. Bill black. Total length 19 inches. Its disposition and needs are the same as the Sulphur–crest's.

LESSER SULPHUR–CRESTED COCKATOO—*CACATUA SULPHUREA*

Distribution: Celebes, Buton and Togian Islands

Adult male: White with a faint yellow tinge on the breast and a more pronounced one on the under surface of the quills and tail. Crest long, pointed and lemon yellow. A yellow patch on the cheeks. Iris practically black. Bill black. Length 13 inches.

Adult female: Has a red iris.

The Lesser Sulphur–crest does not do very well in a cage, but is hardy and enduring in an outdoor aviary, or at liberty. It is very noisy and proves to be quite a good talker. Like all white cockatoos it is easily tamed. The food should be the same as for the Greater Sulphur –crest.

Both sexes sit on the eggs with the male quite as much as, if not more than, the hen. The period of incubation is 24 days. The species breeds well in captivity.

Sulphur-crested Cockatoos resting in the tree tops. This picture was taken in early spring in the mountains of the Great Dividing Range.

rate of its growth. An old pet bird tried to lever a brick out of a drain with its bill and split the upper portion from near the point to the base. I mended the break and in three weeks the split portion had grown down to the point and before the end of the following week no trace of the injury was visible." The Slender–bill Cockatoo compensates for its somewhat grotesque appearance and unmusical voice by an absurd amiability when tamed and a fair capacity for learning to talk. It should be fed on a seed mixture of canary, millet, and oats with as many peanuts as it likes to eat, and any raw vegetables that it cares for. A good–sized turf should be kept in the cage to provide the bird with amusement and exercise for its digging propensities. The Slender–billed Cockatoo is perfectly hardy in an aviary and breeds readily if given the encouragement to

The White Cockatoo is so-called because it displays no colors other than white throughout its body.

Breeding pair of Goffin's Cockatoos with a fledged youngster (lowest). They are exhibiting the threat behavior typical of all cockatoos.

do so. The sexes appear hard to distinguish and I have never seen a bird with a light iris. I concluded that the Slender–bill is one of those cockatoos in which the color of the eye is of no assistance in telling the male from the female.

A pair of these birds I released without special precautions only stayed for a few weeks but it is possible that they would have become more attached to their home had I first let out the male and then the female, alternately, for some months.

GOFFIN'S COCKATOO— *CACATUA GOFFINI*

Distribution: Australia

Adult male: White. bases of the feathers of head and neck, pink. Some pink in front of and below the eye. Crest short. Inner webs of flights and under surface of tail pale yellow. Bill bluish white. Length 16 + inches.

Adult female: Smaller than the male.

The Goffin's Cockatoo, unlike some of its near relatives, appears to be in part, at any rate, a beneficial bird in the wild state, living on the fruit of a creeping, noxious plant called Double–gees whose seed seriously lame sheep. Certain districts in Australia have passed laws protecting the birds, but a wise–acre visiting the district (whose opinions we trust were not heeded) pointed out that the protection was a mistake because whole seeds would probably be voided by the cockatoos and the range of the plant extended. Anybody possessing the most elementary knowledge of a parrot's feeding habits and digestive system would known that the chances of an undigested seed passing through the bird's body are practically nil. Moreover, one would have thought that the thousands of seeds actually assimilated by the cockatoos would, if they had not been eaten, have been a far more likely means of spreading the plant than the one or two supposed to escape destruction! Among birds, it is not seed eaters which are seed distributors, but *berry* eaters.

Three eggs are usually laid, and the nest is situated in a hollow in a tree, cliff–face, or large termite mound. In captivity the Goffin's Cockatoo makes a docile and affectionate pet and a good talker. It can be wintered outdoors, but, like all its family, it is addicted to screaming.

It should be fed like the Gang–gang Cockatoo.

Wild birds have been known to evict sitting Galah

Salmon-crested Cockatoo. A cockatoo will fluff its feathers and raise its crest in play and when aggressive. Be certain you know what mood your cockatoo is in before you approach it. An aggressive cockatoo of this size could harm you.

Macaws

SCARLET MACAW—*ARA MACAO*

Distribution: Mexico and Central America

Adult: Scarlet; feathers of the central part of the wing showing a mixture of red, green, and yellow. Flights and lower edge of the wing blue. Rump pale blue. Some greenish blue and olive feathers at the sides of the rump and on the thighs. Central tail feathers of great length; scarlet with a purplish blue tinge at the base and tips.

A large amount of room is needed to house a macaw. Be certain that the cage used offers enough room for the bird to stretch its wings freely and enough room below the tail so it does not break.

Outer tail feathers blue; some reddish chocolate near the base. Upper mandible whitish. Length 36 inches.

Immatures: Greener on the wings.

The large macaws, of which this gigantic and gaudy bird is a typical example, are easily tamed and have a fair capacity for learning to talk. They are perfectly hardy, can be wintered outdoors, and they are usually fairly safe in mixed company. Among their chief failings are voices in proportion to their size and beaks which only the strongest aviary can resist. There are really only three tolerable ways of keeping macaws—in aviaries, at complete liberty, and with cut wings in enclosures from which they cannot escape by climbing.

The Scarlet Macaw is usually gentle with people and once attached to humans is extremely likely to attack another macaw. It is recorded that an untamed and savage Scarlet Macaw actually killed a Bull Terrier after a combat in which both its wings were broken.

Undoubtedly the Scarlet Macaw shows to best advantage as a liberty bird. In a state of freedom it is said to be far less noisy and destructive than might be expected and tame single birds are reported not to leave the neighborhood of their homes.

Macaws should be fed on a mixture one–half of which consists of peanuts, while canary, hemp, sunflower, oats, and wheat make up the remainder. Plenty of fruit is a necessity. Very young birds benefit from a diet that includes a lot of softfood.

The Scarlet Macaw readily breeds in captivity. A very large barrel partly filled with decayed wood, or a hollow tree trunk, makes the best nest.

GREEN-WINGED MACAW—*ARA CHLOROPTERA*

Distribution: Guatemala to Guiana

Adult: Crimson. Mantle crimson mixed with olive green. Wings olive green

Pair of Scarlet Macaws. Breeding pairs of parrots develop a very close relationship and frequently display moments of true affection and devotion.

mixed with slate blue. Flights blue. Under wing–coverts red. Rump pale blue. Feathers at the sides of the rump tinged with olive. Central tail feathers dark red with blue tips. Outer tail feathers maroon at the base; blue at the tips. Bill horn–white. Total length 34 inches.

A well–known bird, the Green-winged Macaw was imported as early as the end of the 16th century. It is as hardy as other macaws and has the same disposition and needs.

The female is said to be smaller, with a shorter beak.

BLUE AND YELLOW MACAW— *ARA ARARAUNA*

Distribution: Tropical America from Panama to Guiana.

Adult: Blue, darker on the flights and tail. Sides of neck, entire breast, and under wing–coverts yellow. Throat blackish with an outer edging of greyish olive or greenish feathers. Some black feathers on the naked skin of the cheeks. Bill black. Total length 31 inches.

A well–known bird, the Blue and Yellow Macaw is the best talker of the genus, some specimens being very talented. It is perfectly hardy and a good stayer at liberty, with the possible exception of very shy individuals with equally untamed mates. Like many macaws it is capable of blushing when excited, the bare skin of the face becomes suffused with pink.

The Blue and Yellow Macaw breeds freely in captivity and hand-reared specimens make most excellent pets.

The female is said to be smaller, with a shorter and narrower beak.

MILITARY MACAW—*ARA MILITARIS*

Distribution: Mexico, Central and South America

Adult: Olive green, more golden brown on the wings and brighter and bluer on the head. Forehead red. Rump pale blue. Flights and lower edge of the wing blue. Central tail feathers wine red at the base; blue at the tip. Outer tail feathers mainly blue. Bill blackish. Length 27 inches.

The Military Macaw is becoming more popular as a cage bird and pet. It has the ability to say a few words. Treatment as for other large macaws. Hybrids between this species and the Green-Winged Macaw have been known.

The female is said to be smaller, with a shorter and more arched beak though this is not an accurate determination.

Baby Blue and Yellow Macaw. Young birds are easily distinguished by their grey irises and duller colored plumage.

GLAUCOUS MACAW—
ANODORHYNCHUS GLAUCUS

Distribution: Paraguay, Uruguay, and Southern Brazil

Adult: Slate blue, brighter on the rump and very dull on the head, neck and upper breast. A patch of naked yellow skin on the cheek. Bill thick. Total length 29 inches.

A rarely kept bird in captivity resembling other large all–blue macaws in disposition and hardiness.

The Military Macaw is not as popular as some of the other macaw species, however, it is a wonderful bird that enjoys human companionship and does not prove to be as noisy as the other macaw species.

LEAR'S MACAW—
ANODORHYNCHUS LEARI

Distribution: Brazil

Adult: Hyacinth blue. Head and neck paler and more slate colored. Breast feathers with paler tips. Bill black. A patch of naked yellow skin on the cheek. Length 28+ inches.

Lear's Macaw differs from its close ally, the Hyacinth, in

It is not uncommon to find older birds offered for sale due to an owner's death or some other misfortune. Such birds can be very loving and adaptive to a new home, however, they can also be very loud and destructive.

its slightly smaller size and less richly colored head and breast. Unmated birds are

gentle, friendly creatures and, though they can certainly make themselves heard, they screech somewhat less raucously than their partly–colored relatives, their voices have something of the carrion crow timbre about them.

The species is excessively hardy. A bird in my possession, when in rough importation plumage, flew into the tope of a bare oak tree and stayed there for more than 48 hours during a spell of raw January weather. When at length he decided to come down he was not a penny the worse for his long fast and exposure.

Lear's Macaws, like Hyacinth Macaws, are bad stayers at liberty. After a lot of trouble I did manage to induce a couple to settle down

Baby Blue and Yellow Macaw and baby Military Macaw. These two youngsters are captive-bred babies that do not know what it means to be wild. These birds have only known handling, cuddling and love since practically right out of the egg!

Hyacinth Macaw. All parrots are like children; they have their good days and their bad. Caring for a pet parrot is much like caring for a child that will never outgrow toddlerhood.

for some months, but both eventually strayed and were shot. The hen used to gratify her taste for society by flying daily to a town three miles away where she amused herself by pulling out the pegs of people's clothes lines and playing with the dogs. She was sometimes bitten, but such an embarrassing occurrence did not make her any less fond of her canine companions.

HYACINTH MACAW— *ANODORHYNCHUS HYACINTHINUS*

Distribution: Central Brazil
Adult: Deep hyacinth blue. A patch of bare yellow skin at the base of the beak. Bill black and very large. Total length 34 inches.

The Hyacinth Macaw is certainly one of the most remarkable of living birds. Its great size, immense curved beak, and wonderful garb of uniform, deep, hyacinth blue, make it the most elegant of its family. Single birds are very gentle and affectionate, though, as with other macaws and indeed most parrots, the presence of a female companion will often make a male Hyacinth somewhat unfriendly towards humanity. The species is not as hardy as other macaws. It does not take the cold well and should not be kept in an outdoor aviary during the winter months.

SEVERE MACAW—*ARA SEVERA*

Distribution: Brazil, Amazon Valley, Guiana, Colombia, Panama
Adult: Dark green, a bluish tinge on the crown and lower edge of the wing. A dark brown band across the fore-

head and some dark greenish brown feathers on the edge of the cheeks. Outer webs of flights of slate–blue. Under wing–coverts mainly red. Tail reddish brown at the base and on the under surface; remainder blue–green. Bill black. Total length 20 inches.

The smaller macaws have the reputation of being intelligent and affectionate pets with some talent for talking and no worse proclivity for screaming than Amazons. They do quite well in cages if let out for daily exercise.

ILLIGER'S MACAW—*ARA MARACANA*

Distribution: Brazil and Paraguay
Adult male: Dark green. Forehead red. Crown and cheeks bluish; also lower edge of wing. Flights bluish slate.

Some red feathers in the center of the abdomen and on the upper rump. Tail brown and olive at the base; blue green at the tip. Bill horn black. Total length 16+ inches. Smaller than the Severe Macaw.

Adult female: Said to have less red on the forehead.

Immatures: Said to have less red on the forehead and the red patches on the body replaced by yellowish color; upper parts spotted with pale grey–brown.

Illiger's Macaw is said to make a very affectionate pet and a fair talker. It is most playful and amusing. The Illger's Macaw breeds freely in captivity. Like the larger macaws, the small species should be supplied with plenty of soft food when rearing young.

For anyone interested in owning a macaw, the Chestnut-fronted Macaw is nice because it is a smaller version of the other species. It is not a good idea to start in the macaw hobby with a bird of the larger varieties.